Successfully Changing Lives by Building a Community

Easy Steps to Create A Not For Profit Organisation

Anh Vo

Anh Vo

First published 2017

Text copyright 2017 Anh Vo
© Commonwealth of Australia 2014
Photography copyright 2017 Anh Vo
Publisher: Sue Kennedy Publishing

Printed in The United States of America

DEDICATION

To my loving family for all their support. To the Vietnamese community. This book is for you, to open your eyes and ears up to what happens within our community when government funds end up in the wrong hands. I wrote this book so that you know that in most cases people are honest and care for you and everyone in our community. It is to alert you that greed can happen in not just our community but all communities in all countries around the world.
This book has therefore been written to help and show you how to set up and run a not for profit organisation in your local community so that everyone benefits.

Anh Vo

Table of Contents

INTRODUCTION

When we arrived in Australia from a refugee camp in Indonesia, we had nowhere to go to get help, our english accent was not very good so we needed to find a place where we could communicate easily and be able to get the right help quickly and easily. This proved to be quite difficult, as there were no decent associations that we could trust, we stumbled across one that proved to be setup incorrectly under Australian regulations. We found that they were not running the association properly due to many reasons beyond the scope of this book.

I decided that it was time that I wrote this book to help others that may need help in setting up their own associations properly in order to help everyone in their community.

This book is about my personal experience with various associations and realising that there are many out there that have set up associations under the understanding of rules and regulations from their own countries, not realising how the rules and regulations work here in Australia; how the culture here is very different to their own country.

This unfortunately can lead to many problems for people not only from Australia but especially for people from other countries.

Perhaps the message is that the State and Federal Governments in Australia should cease funding to certain associations as it uses taxpayer's money which provides full-time political activities. In all instances, they must work as a charity and be registered with the ACNC.

One of my experiences in particular was with a chapter where all they complained about was the state of the Federal government of Australia and the trouble they had compared to what happened in their own country. It is important to realise that it is not the governments fault. It is your responsibility to understand what happens in this country (Australia) and deal with the rules and regulations in accordance with the constitution of this country.

A good question that should have been asked (with the association I mention above) is "Are you able to take care of all the Vietnam migrants that are currently residing in Australia?" Perhaps this would have resulted in a better outcome?

This book is a reminder to all external auditors that as members of Associations it has been found over the years that there has been misconduct of annual financial reporting which is not accurate or fair to its members.

This book has been written to help people that wish to start a Not for Profit organisation and who do not know where or how to start... It is a guide to help you take the right steps to ensure that your not for profit organisation is setup and runs the correct way so that you can avoid any legal battles.

VIETNAMESE CULTURE

Hoi An Old Town

UNESCO World Heritage Sites in Hoi An

Hoi An, once a major Southeast Asian trading post in the 16th and 17th centuries, is basically a living museum that houses old-town architecture. Some notable heritage buildings include Chinese temples, a Japanese-designed bridge, pagodas, wooden shop-houses, French-colonial houses, and old canals. Although large-scale trading had long moved elsewhere, Hoi An has been successful in preserving and restoring its charming roots and was declared a UNESCO World Heritage site in December 1999.

Vietnamese people have a lovely casual and friendly manner which makes them polite, hospitable, and sensitive. They are very close when it comes to family and friendships are considered very important in their life.

Gift giving is very important in Vietnam because of the significance of the interpersonal relationships within their culture. Therefore, when the Vietnamese offer you a gift they do not like to emphasise the importance or value of the gift, they instead like to pretend that the gift is of no great monetary value even if it is. In Vietnamese culture boasting is criticised, so they avoid making a big deal about it.

The Vietnamese are proud people who like to recite to a myth that they are descendants of an angel and a dragon, having 4000 years of civilisation.

The language is made up of around 60% modern Vietnamese words that of Chinese origin. Many of the basic words like geographical terms have been adopted from mono tonal Mon-Khmer languages and the tonality comes from Tai.

Banh Chung is one of many special traditional foods that the Vietnamese people enjoy as part of their New Year's celebrations.
Xoan singing is a folk cultural product of Phu Tho province that was last sung in communal houses in villages back in the spring of 1945.

The conical hat of Vietnam first came to be around in the 13th century during the Tran Dynasty according to ancient documents.

Ha Long Bay, located in the Gulf of Tonkin, within Quang Ninh Province, in the northeast of Vietnam, is 165 km from the capital of Ha Noi. Covering an area of 43,400 ha and including over 1600 islands and islets, most of which are uninhabited and unaffected by humans, it forms a spectacular seascape of limestone pillars and is an ideal model of a mature Karst landscape developed during a warm and wet tropical climate. The property's exceptional scenic beauty is complemented by its great biological interest.

Vietnamese religion

Shamanism

A shaman is best described as an intermediary between humankind and the spirit world. They possess the ability to communicate with the spirit world in such a way as to dispel evil, to explain the turns of fate, and to transmit instructions from the spirits.

Although shamanism exists in mainstream religion in Vietnam, it is mostly found in the traditions of the country's ethnic minority groups, many of whom retain a shaman in each village. To invoke the spirits, a shaman uses songs and dances, spells and talismans leading to the induction of a trance-like state during which he or she is in direct contact with spirits.

In theory, such activities are labelled as superstition and are illegal. However, the law is largely ignored, and even the authorities recognise the tourism potential of such rituals. One example of this is a traditional annual festival where they slaughter a buffalo as a sacrifice to the spirits. This terrible spectacle is now being promoted by the tourism department of the area and has become very popular.

Taoism

In Vietnam, Taoism is the linking mechanism for Buddhism, Confucianism, Ancestor worship and animism. Countless images of the Gods of Taoism are in temples and pagodas throughout the country. Most homes use their altar to worship the 'Kitchen God', the name for the triumvirate of Taoist deities that monitor the families' behavior. Many of Vietnam's festivals, including Tet, have a Taoist tradition.

Fortune-telling, astrology and geomancy are an accepted part of everyday life. Ingredients for traditional medicine and foods are designated as 'hot' or 'cool', and the principle of harmony and balance underpins healthcare.

Visitors to Vietnam will often be puzzled by a small mirrored octagonal disc, with the Yin Yang and other symbols, fixed above the door of most houses and small shops. It is to guard the house by barring wandering spirits, or ghosts.

Confucianism

Confucianism was firmly implanted in Vietnam during the thousand years of its occupation by China and mirrored its development. As in China, an intellectual elite developed, and the principles of obedience and respect for education and authority were instilled throughout society, profoundly influencing the family structure and creating a tightly defined social hierarchy.

In Hanoi in 1070, the establishment of the Van Mieu (Temple of Literature), a temple of learning dedicated to Confucius, marked the emergence of Confucianism as a cult. Like China, it reached a peak during the 15th century – the 'golden age' of King Le Thanh Tong, then steadily decayed into decadence and corruption opening the door for the French invasion.

Christianity

Christianity was introduced to Vietnam in the 16th century by missionaries from Europe's main Catholic evangelist countries, France, Spain and Portugal. One of the early arrivals was Alexandre de Rhodes, a French Jesuit who greatly impressed the Trinh lords who ruled the north at that time, thus easing the way for permanent missions in Hanoi, Danang and Hoi An.

Buddhism

Historically, most Vietnamese have identified themselves with Buddhism, which originated in what is now southern Nepal around 530 B.C. as an offshoot of Hinduism. Its founder was Gautama, a prince who bridled at the formalism of Hinduism as it was being interpreted by the priestly caste of Brahmans. Gautama spent years meditating and wandering as an ascetic until he discovered the path of enlightenment to nirvana, the world of endless serenity in which one is freed from the cycle of birth, death, and rebirth.

According to Buddhist thought, human salvation lies in discovering the "four noble truths"–that man is born to suffer in successive lives, that the cause of this suffering is man's craving for earthly pleasures and possessions, that the suffering ceases upon his deliverance from this craving, and that he achieves this deliverance by following "the noble eightfold path."

The foundation of the Buddhist concept of morality and right behavior, the eightfold path, consists of right views, or sincerity in leading a religious life; right intention, or honesty in judgment; right speech, or sincerity in speech; right conduct, or sincerity in work; right livelihood, or sincerity in making a living; right effort, or sincerity in aspiration; right mindfulness, or sincerity in memory; and right concentration, or sincerity in meditation.

The Vietnamese Pancake (Bánh xèo)

Bánh xèo *[băŋ sêw], literally "sizzling cake", named for the loud sizzling sound it makes when the rice batter is poured into the hot skillet is a Vietnamese savoury fried pancake made of rice flour, water, turmeric powder, stuffed with slivers of fatty pork, shrimp, diced green onion, and bean sprouts.*

Vietnamese Culture

Traditionally in Vietnam children live with their parents until they get married. The extended family arrange the marriage and the individuals are then consulted of their choice of mate. A typical engagement lasts around six months where there is little contact between the couple prior to the marriage. Once married, they move to the husbands father's house.

Vietnamese men marry between the ages of 20 and 30 and the women between 18 to 25. Vietnamese women keep their maiden names legally, however they use their husband's name on formal occasions.

The Vietnamese have titles of respect when it comes to how you address people formally. They use Mr or Ms or a title plus their first name. Some of the titles are not used in English. A show of respect is to add "Thua" (meaning please) in front of the first name.

In Vietnamese tradition people use their family name first, then their middle name,

11

and then their first (given) name last.

Vietnamese do not usually have physical contact with each other and women do not shake hands with other women or men. The way Vietnamese greet is by slightly bowing to each other, sometimes they can join hands. It is usual for higher ranking people to greeted first, meaning the head of the family.

In Vietnamese culture there is little concern about wealth, it is more concerned about status for example what you have obtained with age and education.

It is important not to speak in a loud tone or with excessive gestures as this is considered very rude, especially if it is a Vietnamese women.

The elderly as well as the parents of families are taken care of by the children until death. Insults to the elders or ancestors are seen as very serious and will often lead to severed social ties.

It is very disrespectful to touch another person's head, the only people that can touch the head of a child is an elder.

When you invite someone out for an outing in Vietnam, the bill is always paid for by the person offering the invitation.

When you have a meeting with a Vietnamese person, it is customary for them to turn up late as they do not want to be seen overly enthusiastic.

It is important not to break your promise with the Vietnamese as this is seen as a serious violation of social expectation and to regain the confidence in the relationship is very difficult.

Vietnamese Food Recipes

This dish is usually served with a special sauce made from soy sauce and breads. It can also be eaten with steamed rice, pickled green cabbage, fish sauce and a little chilli if desired. This is especially good on cold days.

Discover the true flavour of Vietnamese people in the morning through one of their stunning recipes which is a Mixture of Salty Steamed Sticky Rice (Xôi Mặn Thập Cẩm)

Beef in Lemon Juice Recipe (Bò Tái Chanh)

Anh Vo

LIFE IN VIETNAM

Vietnam is a poor, densely populated country that has historically been associated with war and a punishing centrally planned economy. Today, it is becoming more of a tourist destination with its beautiful countryside and beaches.

Vietnam is a relatively small country that covers a total area of approximately 329,500 square kilometres. It is home to around 54 different ethnic groups. The most significant group is that of the Kinh (Viet) people, who account for 86% of the total population. The country is divided into 58 provinces and there are 5 centrally-controlled municipalities existing at the same level as the provinces. These are known as Hanoi, Hai Phong, Da Nang, Ho Chi Minh City, and Can Tho.

Vietnam has a comparatively low cost of living and can live a comfortable life with moderate expenditure. There is a variety of accommodation available to suit all budgets that include up market apartments in the major cities to modest houses in the outer suburbs.

Our family and all Vietnamese people live under poor conditions and are unable to afford all foods and medicine, this is controlled by Communist revolution members and armed forces. To understand these circumstances, it is important to know how and why the war in Vietnam began:

Complex of Hué Monuments

Established as the capital of unified Viet Nam in 1802, Hué was not only the political but also the cultural and religious centre under the Nguyen dynasty until 1945. The Perfume River winds its way through the Capital City, the Imperial City, the Forbidden Purple City and the Inner City, giving this unique feudal capital a setting of great natural beauty.

The Complex of Hue Monuments is a UNESCO World Heritage Site and is located in the city of Hue in central Vietnam. Hue was founded as the Vietnam capital city by Gia Long, the first king of the Nguyen Dynasty in 1802. It held this position for nine Nguyen dynasties until 1945.

In 1858, France launched an attack on Đà Nẵng, starting its invasion of Vietnam. In 1867, France completed its conquest of southern Vietnam (Cochinchina), comprising the provinces of Biên Hòa, Gia Định, Định Tường, Vĩnh Long, An Giang, and Hà Tiên. To consolidate the newly established colony, on 23 February 1868, Lagrandière, Governor of Cochinchina, held a ceremony to lay the foundation stone of a new palace to replace the old wooden palace built in 1863. The new palace was designed by Charles Hermite, who was also the architect of the Hong Kong City Hall. The first cubic stone, measuring 50 cm along each edge, with indentations containing French gold and silver coins bearing Napoleon III's effigy, came from Biên Hòa.

The complex covered an area of 12 hectares, including a palace with an 80-meter-wide façade, a guest-chamber capable of accommodating 800 people, with a spacious gardens covered by green trees and a lawn. Most of the building materials were imported from France. Owing to the Franco-Prussian War of 1870, construction fell behind schedule and was not completed until 1873. The palace was named **Norodom Palace** after the then king of Cambodia, Norodom (1834–1904). The avenue in front of the palace bore the same name. From 1871 to 1887, the palace was used by the French Governor of Cochinchina (*Gouverneur de la Cochinchine*); therefore, it was referred to as the **Governor's Palace**. From 1887 to 1945, all Governors-General of French Indochina used the palace as their residence and office. The office of the Cochinchinese Governors was relocated to a nearby villa.

On May 7, 1954, France surrendered to the Việt Minh after its defeat at the Battle of Điện Biên Phủ. France agreed to sign the Geneva Accords and withdrew its troops from Vietnam. According to the accords, Vietnam would be divided pending general elections. The 17th Parallel would act as the temporary border until a vote based on universal suffrage was held to establish a unified Vietnamese government. North Vietnam was under the control of the

Việt Minh communists, while South Vietnam was under the anti-communist State of Vietnam. On 7 September 1954, Norodom Palace was handed over to the prime minister of the State of Vietnam, Ngô Đình Diệm by a representative of the French presence in Vietnam, General Paul Ély.

Main articles: 1962 South Vietnamese Independence Palace bombing, Arrest and assassination of Ngô Đình Diệm, and 1963 South Vietnamese coup

On 27 February 1962, two pilots of Diệm's Vietnam Air Force, Nguyễn Văn Cử and Phạm Phú Quốc, rebelled and flew two A-1 Skyraider (A-1D/AD-6 variant) aircraft towards the palace and bombed it, instead of going on a raid against the Việt Cộng. As a result, almost the entire left wing was destroyed. However, Diệm and his family escaped the assassination attempt. As it was almost impossible to restore the palace, Diệm ordered it demolished and commissioned a new building in its place. The new palace was constructed according to a design by Ngô Viết Thụ, a Vietnamese architect[1] who won the First Grand Prize of Rome (Grand Prix de Rome) in 1955, the highest recognition of the Beaux-Arts school in Paris. He was also a laureate of the Rome Architecture Award.

The construction of the new Independence Palace started on 1 July 1962. Meanwhile, Diệm and his ruling family moved to Gia Long Palace (today the Ho Chi Minh City Museum). However, Diệm did not see the completed hall as he and his brother and chief adviser Ngô Đình Nhu were assassinated after a *coup d'état* led by General Dương Văn Minh in November 1963. The completed hall was inaugurated on 31 October 1966 by the chairman of the National Leadership Committee, General Nguyễn Văn Thiệu, who was then the head of a military junta. The Independence Hall served as Thiệu's home and office from October 1967 to 21 April 1975, when he fled[2] the country as communist North Vietnamese forces swept southwards in the decisive Ho Chi Minh Campaign.

On 8 April 1975, Nguyễn Thanh Trung, a pilot of the Vietnam Air Force and an undetected communist spy, flew an F-5E aircraft from Biên Hòa Air Base to bomb the palace, but caused no significant damage. At 10:45 on 30 April 1975, a tank of the North Vietnamese Army bulldozed through the main gate, ending the Vietnam War.

In November 1975, after the negotiation convention between the communist North Vietnam and their colleagues in South Vietnam was completed, the Provisional Revolutionary Government renamed the palace **Reunification Hall** (*Hội trường Thống Nhất*).

The Palace is depicted on the 200-đồng note of the Republic of Vietnam.

Source: Wikipedia

First Indochina War

In the First Indochina War, the Viet Minh, supported the People's Republic of China and the Soviet Union, they fought to gain their independence from the French, supported initially by the remaining troops of the Japanese Army after its surrender to Britain, also by the French-loyalist Vietnamese catholic minority, and later by the United States in the frame of the Cold War. This war of independence lasted from December 1946 until July 1954, with most of the fighting taking place in areas surrounding Hanoi. It ended with the French defeat at the Battle of Dien Bien Phu and French withdrawal from Vietnam after the Geneva Agreements.

Negotiations between the French and Ho Chi Minh led to an agreement in March 1946 that appeared to promise a peaceful solution. Under the agreement, France recognised the Viet Minh government and gave Vietnam the status of a free state within the French Union. The French troops remained in Vietnam, but they were withdrawn progressively over five years. For a period in early 1946, the French cooperated with Ho Chi Minh as he consolidated the Viet Minh's dominance over other nationalist groups, in particular those politicians who were backed by the Chinese Nationalist Party.

Despite tactical cooperation between the French and the Viet Minh, their policies were irreconcilable: the French aimed to re-establish colonial rule, while Hanoi wanted total independence. French intentions were revealed in the decision of Georges-Thierry d'Argenlieu, the high commissioner for Indochina, to proclaim Cochinchina an autonomous republic in June 1946.

Further negotiations did not resolve the basic differences between the French and the Viet Minh. In late November 1946 the French naval vessels bombarded Haiphong, causing several thousand civilian casualties; the subsequent Viet Minh attempt to overwhelm French troops in Hanoi in December was generally considered to be the beginning of the First Indochina War.

Initially, confident of victory, the French long ignored the real political cause of the war and the desire of the Vietnamese people, including their anticommunist leaders, to achieve unity and independence for their country. French efforts to deal with those issues were devious and ineffective.

The French reunited Cochinchina with the rest of Vietnam in 1949, proclaiming the Associated State of Vietnam, and appointed the former emperor Bao Dai as chief of state. Most nationalists, however, denounced these maneuvers, and leadership in the struggle for independence from the French remained with the Viet Minh.

Meanwhile, the Viet Minh waged an increasingly successful guerrilla war, aided after 1949 by the new communist government of China. The United States, fearful of the spread of communism in Asia, sent large amounts of aid to the French. The French, however, were shaken by the fall of their garrison at Dien Bien Phu in May 1954 and agreed to negotiate an end to the war at an international conference in Geneva.

Second Vietnam war : Indochina during World War II

Ho Chi Minh returned to Vietnam from France and helped to create the Viet Minh national independence coalition in 1941. A founding member of the French Communist Party, Ho Chi Minh had de-emphasised his communist ties and dissolved the Indochinese Communist Party, in order to unite the country.

When the Vietnamese famine broke out in 1945 causing 2 million deaths, after French and Japanese colonial administration continued to export food to France in a post war economy, the Viet Minh arranged a massive relief effort, consolidating popular support for their nationalist cause. Ho Chi Minh was elected Prime Minister of the Viet Minh in 1945.

When World War II ended, the August Revolution expelled the Japanese colonial army and gave control of the country to Viet Minh. The Japanese surrendered to the Chinese Nationalists in North Vietnam. Emperor Bao Dai abdicated power to the Viet Minh, on August 25, 1945. In a popular move, Ho Chi Minh made Bao Dai "supreme adviser" to the Viet Minh-led government in Hanoi, which asserted its independence on September 2 as the Democratic Republic of Vietnam (DRV) and issued a Proclamation of Independence of the Democratic Republic of Vietnam. In 1946, Vietnam had its first constitution.

In 1948, France tried to regain its colonial control over Vietnam. In South Vietnam, the Japanese had surrendered to British forces, who had supported the Free French in fighting the Viet Minh, along with the armed religious Cao Dai and Hoa Hao sects and the Binh Xuyen organised crime group. The French re-installed Bao Dai as the head of state of Vietnam, which now comprised of central and southern Vietnam. The ensuing war, between the French-controlled South and the independent Communist-allied North, is known as the First Indochina War. It ended in a resounding defeat of the French Colonial Troops (Troupes colonials) by the People's Army of Vietnam at Dien Bien Phu, which marked the first time that a European colonial Army was defeated in pitched battle.

Vietnam war

A large section of rubble is all that remained in this one block square area of Saigon on Feb. 5, 1968, after fierce Tet Offensive fighting. Rockets and grenades, combined with fires, laid waste to the area. An Quang Pagoda, location of Viet Cong headquarters during the fighting, is at the top of the photo. (AP Photo/Johner)

Second Indochina War

The Second Indochina War, commonly known as the Vietnam War, pitted the recently successful Communist Vietnam People's Army (VPA or PAVN, but also incorrectly known as the North Vietnamese Army or NVA) and the National Front for the Liberation of Vietnam (South Vietnamese NLF guerrilla fighters allied with the PAVN, known in the Republic of Vietnam as the Viet Cong, meaning 'Communists Traitor to Vietnam') against United States troops and the United States-backed ARVN (Republic of Vietnam soldiers).

During the War, the North Vietnamese transported most of their supplies via the Ho Chi Minh Trail (known to the Vietnamese as the Truong Son Trail, after the Truong Son mountains), which ran through Laos and Cambodia. As a result, the areas of these nations bordering Vietnam would see heavy combat during the war.

For the United States, the political and combat goals were ambiguous: success and progress were ill-defined and, along with the large numbers of casualties, the Vietnam War raised moral issues that made the war increasingly unpopular at home. U.S. news reports of the 1968 Tet offensive, especially from CBS, were unfavorable in regard to the lack of progress in ending the war. Although the 1968 Tet offensive resulted in a military victory for South Vietnam and the United States, with virtually complete destruction of the NLF forces combat capability, it was, by the intensity of the combats, the contradiction it implied with recent reports of withdrawals of US troops and status of the war, also a turning point in American voter opposition to U.S. support for their Cold War Vietnamese allies.

The United States began withdrawing troops from Vietnam in 1970, with the last troops returning in January 1973. The Paris Peace Accords called for a cease-fire, and prohibited the North Vietnamese from sending more troops into South Vietnam - although the North Vietnamese were permitted to continue to occupy those regions of South Vietnam they had conquered in the 1972 Easter Offensive.

The North Vietnamese never intended to abide by the agreement. Fighting continued sporadically through 1973 and 1974, while the North Vietnamese planned a major offensive, tentatively scheduled for 1976. The North Vietnamese Army in South Vietnam had been ravaged during the Easter offensive in 1973, and it was projected that it would take until 1976 to rebuild their logistical capabilities.

The withdrawal had catastrophic effects on the South Vietnamese Army (ARVN). Shortly after the Paris Peace Accords, the United States Congress made major budget cuts in military aid to the South Vietnamese. The ARVN, which had been trained by American troops to use American tactics, quickly fell into disarray. Although it remained an effective fighting force throughout 1973 and 1974, by January 1975 it had disintegrated. The North Vietnamese hurriedly attacked the much weakened South, and met with little resistance.

Saigon, the capital of South Vietnam, was taken by the PAVN on April 30, 1975, and the Second Indochina War ended.

During the Second Vietnam War, I was a member of one million South Vietnamese Arm Force (MILITARY) who protected the South Vietnamese population and land, we went into battle with North Vietnamese Communist (VC) armed forces that were attached to the South.

Below is a list of who won and lost their lives or were wounded in the Vietnam War:

South Vietnam	North Vietnam & Viet Cong
195,000–430,000 Civilians dead: 220,357 Military dead: 313,000 Wounded: 1,170,000	Civilians dead: 65,000 Military dead or missing: 444,000 – 1,100,000 Wounded: 600,000+
United States Dead: 58,315 Wounded: 303,644	**China** Dead: 1,100 Wounded: 4,200
South Korea Dead: 5,099 Wounded: 10,962 Missing: 4	**Soviet Union** Dead: 16
Australia Dead: 500 Wounded: 3,129	**North Korea** Dead: 14
Thailand Dead: 351 Wounded: 1,358	
New Zealand Dead: 37 Wounded: 187	
Philippines Dead: 9 Wounded: 64	
Total Dead: 479,668 – 807,311 **Total Wounded: 1,490,000+**	**Total Dead: 455,476 – 1,170,476** **Total Wounded: 608,200**

Vietnamese civilians death toll: 260,000–2,000,000

Cambodian Civil War death toll: 200,000–300,000

Laotian Civil War death toll: 20,000–200,000

Total civilian death toll: 480,000–2,500,000

Total death toll: 1,484,000–3,886,026

For more information, see Vietnam War casualties and Aircraft losses of the Vietnam War
* indicates approximations, see Casualties below

** This figure includes all of the dead from the Laotian and Cambodian civil wars.

-Source Wikipedia

Dated 30 April, the Fall of Saigon, Capital of the Republic of South Vietnamese government: the Vietnam war ends after 30 years.

What happened after the war ended:

Re-education camp is the official title given to the prison camps operated by the Communist government of Vietnam following the end of the Vietnam War. In such "re-education camps", the government imprisoned over 1 million former military officers, government workers and supporters of the former government of South Vietnam. Re-education as it was implemented in Vietnam was seen as both a means of revenge and as a sophisticated technique of repression and indoctrination, which developed following the 1975 Fall of Saigon. An estimated 1 million people were imprisoned with no formal charges or trials. According to published academic studies in the United States and Europe, 165,000 people died in the Socialist Republic of Vietnam's re-education camps. Thousands were tortured or abused. Prisoners were incarcerated for as long as 17 years, with most terms ranging from three to 10 years.

The term 're-education camp' is also used to refer to prison camps operated by the People's Republic of China during the Cultural Revolution, or to the laogai and laojiao camps currently operated by the Chinese government. The theory underlying such camps is the Maoist theory of reforming counter-revolutionaries into socialist citizens by re-education through labor.

After the fall of Saigon on April 30, 1975, hundreds of thousands of South Vietnamese men, from former officers in the armed forces, to religious leaders, to employees of the Americans or the old government, were rounded up in re-education camps to "learn about the ways of the new government." They were never tried, judged or convicted of any crime. Many South Vietnamese men chose to flee on boats, but others had established lives with loved ones in Vietnam, so they did not flee, but entered these camps in hope of quickly reconciling with the new government and continuing their lives peacefully.

The hundreds of thousands of Vietnamese who were imprisoned in re-education camps from 1975 basically fell into two categories:

1) Those who were detained in re-education camps from 1975 because they collaborated with the other side during the war, and

2) Those who were arrested in the years after 1975 for attempting to exercise such democratic freedoms as those mentioned in Article 11 of the 1973 Paris Agreements. In other words, both categories of prisoners were held in direct violation of Article 11 of the 1973 Paris Agreements, an international treaty, and therefore of international law.

Officially, the Vietnamese government does not consider the re-education camps to be prisons, but rather places where individuals could be rehabilitated into society through education and socially constructive labor.

The Hanoi government defended the re-education camps by placing the "war criminal" label on the prisoners. A 1981 memorandum of the Socialist Republic of Vietnam to Amnesty International claimed that all those in the re-education camps were guilty of acts of national treason as defined in Article 3 of the 30 October 1967 Law on Counter-revolutionary Crimes (enacted for the government of North Vietnam), which specifies punishments ranging from 20 years to life in prison or the death penalty. However, it was instead allowing the prisoners to experience "re-education," which is applied in Vietnam because Vietnam says it is the most "humanitarian" system and because it is the most advantageous punishment for law breakers.

Registration and arrest

In May 1975, specific groups of Vietnamese were ordered to register with the new government that had established control over the South on April 30, 1975. Then, in June, the new government issued orders instructing those who had registered in May to report to various places for re-education. Soldiers, non-commissioned officers and rank-and-file personnel of the former South Vietnamese government were to undergo a three-day "reform study" from June 11–13, which they would attend during the day and they would go home at night.

The others who had been ordered to report for "reform study" were not allowed the same arrangement of attending during the day and going home at night, but were instead to be confined to their sites of "reform study" until the course ended.

Nevertheless, there was some hope, for the government gave the clear impression that reform study would last no more than a month for even the highest-ranking officers and officials of the former government in South Vietnam, and ten days for lower-ranking officers and officials.

Thus, officers of the Army of the Republic of Vietnam (ARVN) forces from the rank of second lieutenant to captain, along with low-ranking police officers and intelligence cadres, were ordered to report to various sites, bringing along "enough paper, pens, clothes, mosquito nets, personal effects, food or money to last ten days beginning from the day of their arrival."

High- ranking military and police officers of the ARVN, from major to general, along with mid and high-ranking intelligence officers, members of the ARVN executive, judicial and legislative branches, including all elected members of the House of Representatives and the Senate, and, finally, leaders of "reactionary" (i.e. non-communist) political parties in South Vietnam, were ordered to report to various sites bringing enough "paper, pens, clothes, mosquito-nets, personal effects, food or money to last a month beginning from the day of their first meeting."

The new government announced that there would be three days of re-education for ARVN soldiers, ten days for low-ranking officers and officials, and one month for high-ranking ARVN officers and officials. Many teachers reported for re-education, assuming that they would have to undergo it sooner or later anyway. Sick people also reported for re-education, assured by the government that there would be doctors and medical facilities in the schools and that the patients would be well treated.

Indoctrination and forced confessions

During the early phase of re-education, lasting from a few weeks to a few months, inmates were subjected to intensive political indoctrination. Subjects' studies included the exploitation by American imperialism of workers in other countries, the glory of labor, the inevitable victory of Vietnam, led by the Communist Party, over the U.S., and the generosity of the new government toward the "rebels" (those who fought on the other side during the war).

Another feature emphasized during the early stage of re-education, but continued throughout one's imprisonment, was the confession of one's alleged misdeeds in the past. All prisoners in the camps were required to write confessions, no matter how trivial their alleged crimes might have been. Mail clerks, for example, were told that they were guilty of aiding the "puppet war machinery" through circulating the mail, while religious chaplains were found guilty of providing spiritual comfort and encouragement to enemy troops.

The work

In the re-education camps much emphasis was placed on "productive labor." Such labor was described by SRV spokesman Hoang Son as "absolutely necessary" for re-education because "under the former government, they (the prisoners) represented the upper strata of society and got rich under U.S. patronage. They could scorn the working people. Now the former social order was turned upside down, and after they finished their stay in camps they had to earn their living by their own labour and live in a society where work was held in honor." Thus, in the eyes of the Vietnamese rulers, "productive labor" was a necessary aspect in the overturning of the social order. Yet in examining the conditions under which this labor took place, it seems that there was also an element of revenge.

The labor was mostly hard physical work, some of it very dangerous, such as mine field sweeping. No technical equipment was provided for this extremely risky work, and as a result, many prisoners were killed or wounded in mine field explosions. Other kinds of work included cutting trees, planting corn and root crops, clearing the jungle, digging wells, latrines and garbage pits, and constructing barracks within the camp and fences around it. The inmates were generally organised into platoons and work units, where they were forced to compete with each other for better records and work achievements.

This often pushed inmates to exhaustion and nervousness with each person and group striving to surpass or at least fulfill the norms set by camp authorities, or they would be classified as 'lazy' and ordered to do 'compensation work' on Sundays. North Vietnamese children were brought in to routinely pester prisoners, teenage girls stomping on the bare feet of former army officers as they marched to work. Sometimes prisoners who missed their quota were shackled and placed in solitary confinement cells.

Deaths from starvation and disease occurred frequently and bodies were often buried in graves on site, which were later abandoned. The work was done in the hot tropical sun, by prisoners who were poorly nourished and received little or no medical care. The poor health, combined with hard work, mandatory confessions and political indoctrination, made life very difficult for prisoners in Vietnam, and contributed to a high death rate in the camps.

Former prisoners describe the constant hunger that resulted from a lack of food while they were in the camps. The government deliberately kept the prisoners on low rations. The lack of food caused severe malnutrition for many prisoners and weakened their resistance to various diseases. Most common among the diseases were malaria, beriberi and dysentery. Tuberculosis was also widespread in some of the camps. Medical supplies were generally nonexistent in the camps and medical care was very inadequate, usually limited to a poorly trained medic and perhaps a few prisoners who had formerly been medical doctors. The result was a high death rate from diseases.

Rules and regulations

The authorities sought to maintain strict control over the thoughts of the prisoners, and forbade prisoners from keeping and reading books or magazines of the former government, reminiscing in conversation about "imperialism and the puppet south," singing old patriotic and love songs from the former government, discussing political questions (outside authorised discussions), harboring "reactionary" thoughts or possessing "superstitious" beliefs.

It has been acknowledged by Hanoi that violence has in fact been directed against the prisoners, although it maintains that these are isolated cases and not indicative of general camp policy. Former prisoners, on the other hand, report frequent beatings for minor infractions, such as missing work because of illness. Violations of rules led to various forms of punishment, including being tied up in contorted positions, shackled in conex boxes or dark cells, forced to work extra hours or receiving reduced food rations.

Many prisoners were beaten, some to death, or subjected to very harsh forms of punishment due to the cruelty of certain camp officials and guards. Some were executed, especially for attempting to escape. It was also forbidden to be impolite to the cadres of the camp, and this rule was sometimes abused to the point where the slightest indication of a lack of deference to the cadres had been interpreted as rudeness and was therefore harshly punished.

Longtime anti-Vietnam war and human rights activist Ginetta Sagan described conditions in the camps in 1982:

During the last three years, friends and I have interviewed several hundred former prisoners, read newspaper articles on the camps as well as various reports of Amnesty International, and have studied official statements from the Vietnamese Government and its press on the re-education camps. The picture that emerges is one of severe hardship, where prisoners are kept on a starvation diet, overworked and harshly punished for minor infractions of camp rules. We know of cases where prisoners have been beaten to death, confined to dark cells or in ditches dug around the perimeters of the camps and executed for attempting escape.

A common form of punishment is confinement to the CONEX boxes, air-freight containers that were left behind by the United States in 1975. The boxes vary in size; some are made of wood and others of metal. In a CONEX box that is 4 feet high and 4 feet wide, for example, several prisoners would be confined with their feet shackled, and allowed only one bowl of rice and water a day. "*It reminded me of the pictures I saw of Nazi camp inmates after World War II,*" said a physician we interviewed who witnessed the release of four prisoners who had been confined to a CONEX box for one month. None of them survived."

Visitation

As of 1980, official regulations stated that prisoners in the camps could be visited by their immediate family once every three months. Family visits were important, not only because of the personal need for prisoners and their loved ones to have contact with each other, but also because the families could bring food to their relatives in some of the camps. It has been reported that the prisoners in these camps would not have survived without such food.

The duration of the visits were not long, reported by former prisoners to last from 15 to 30 minutes. Moreover, family visits would be suspended for prisoners who broke the rules, and it has also been said that only families who had proven their loyalty to the government were allowed visiting privileges.

Most of the former prisoners interviewed have been in between three and five different re-education camps. It is believed that the movement of prisoners from one camp to another was intended to prevent both the inmates and their relatives from knowing a specific camp's real location. That way, escapes from prison could be prevented, and prisoners' relatives could be prevented from visiting them.

The release of prisoners

In June 1976, the Provisional Revolutionary Government of South Vietnam, in one of its last policy announcements before the official reunification of Vietnam, stated that those in the camps would either be tried or released after three years of imprisonment. But this promise was broken. The policy announced that those still in the camps would stay there for three years, but would be released early if they made "real progress, confess their crimes and score merits".

Since there was no clear criteria for releasing the inmates from the camps, bribery and family connections with high-ranking officials were more likely to speed up release than the prisoner's good behavior.

Released prisoners were put on probation and placed under surveillance for six months to one year, and during that time they had no official status, no exit visas, no access to government food rations and no right to send their children to school.

If the progress of the former prisoners was judged unsatisfactory during this period, they could be fired from their jobs, put under surveillance for another six months to a year, or sent back to the re-education camps. Faced with these challenges, many chose to flee the country and became boat people.

Some prisoners who had been imprisoned since the Fall of Saigon were released as recently as the year 2000. " It also said that some Vietnamese would be brought to trial, including those who deserted the NLF during the war, those who owed "many blood debts" to the people and those who fled to "foreign countries with their U.S. masters."

The U.S. government considers re-education camp inmates to be political prisoners. In 1989, the Reagan administration entered into an agreement with the Vietnamese government, pursuant to which Vietnam would free all former ARVN soldiers and officials held in re-education camps and allow them to emigrate to the United States. Thus began the third large influx of Vietnamese immigrants into the country.

Camp Conditions and Deaths

In most of the re-education camps, living conditions were inhumane. Prisoners were treated with little food, poor sanitation, and no medical care. They were also assigned to do hard and risky work such as clearing the jungle, constructing barracks, digging wells, cutting trees and even mine field sweeping without necessary working equipment.

Although that hard work required a lot of energy, their provided food portions were extremely small. As a prisoner recall, the experience of hunger dominated every man in his camp. Food was the only thing they talked about. Even when they were quiet, food still haunted their thoughts, their sleep and their dreams. Worse still, various diseases such as malaria, beriberi and dysentery were widespread in some of the camps. As many prisoners were weakened by the lack of food, those diseases could now easily take away their lives.

Starvation diet, overwork, diseases and harsh punishment resulted in a high death rate of the prisoners. According to academic studies of American researchers, a total of 165,000 Vietnamese people died in those camps.

Source: Wikipedia

My story of those times:

I was a sadly one of the ONE MILLION VICTIMS OF THE "RE- EDUCATION CAMPS." Luckily, I was released in August 1981 and then on 24 October 2012 I was able to escape out of the country by boat . Our boat was 10m long and 3m wide it had a 2 cylinder engine and carried 58 people including my wife and two children.

After 3 days and four nights we landed on the Indonesian border of an Island named Terampa. We stayed at Terampa Island for one week. From there an Indonesian Navy ship took us to KUKU Island under the United Nation of Refugees to process our documents so we could stay in KUKU for 30 days. We then got transferred to Galang Island while we waited for an Australian Delegation interview, thankfully it was processed with all the legal documents we needed and our family was accepted by the Political Refugee Visa.

My wife, two children and I arrived in Melbourne on 23 September 1984 and settled into our new life. I have never been back to visit Vietnam, I vowed I would never live like that again under a communist regime.

There are many times I shed a tear to this day as I miss my parents, my system and my brother who sadly passed away and I was unable to attend his funeral.

I really miss my younger brother, we used to share a sweet potato when we were hungry, hold each other when were cold. He is the only family I still have alive in Vietnam, I miss him very much.

THE UNLUCKY VIETNAMESE

Terror in Little Saigon
California - USA

The following is an excerpt from The Front - Terror in Little Saigon by ProPublica

https://www.propublica.org/article/terror-in-little-saigon-vietnam-american-journalists-murdered

Part I

His name was Hoang Co Minh. He had a mess of thinning, coal-black hair and a caterpillar mustache. It was 1983, and Minh had come to a packed convention center in Washington, D.C., to make an announcement: He intended to reconquer Vietnam.

Minh, a former officer in the South Vietnamese Navy, told the assembled crowd that he'd built a force that would topple the Hanoi government and liberate his homeland from the totalitarian rule of the Communists.

The crowd — thousands of Vietnamese refugees who'd fled the country after Saigon fell in 1975 — erupted in celebration, and in some cases, tears of joy. Clad in black, a long plaid scarf draped around his neck, Minh smiled broadly and let the audience's ecstatic reaction wash over him. Video of the event shows Minh thrusting both hands into the air and waving like a head of state.

Minh had started his guerilla army a few years earlier. It was called the National United Front for the Liberation of Vietnam. The group had established a base in the wilds of Southeast Asia — a secret location within striking distance of Vietnam —

and built a network of chapters across the U.S that raised money for the coming invasion.

Those U.S. chapters, it seems, had already opened what amounted to a second front, this one in America: Front members used violence to silence Vietnamese Americans who dared question the group's politics or aims. Calling for normalized relations with the Communist victors back home was enough to merit a beating or, in some cases, a death sentence.

FBI agents eventually opened a domestic terrorism investigation into the Front's activities. Thousands of pages of newly declassified FBI records obtained by ProPublica and Frontline show that the agents came to suspect that Minh's group had orchestrated the killing of Vietnamese-American journalists, as well as a wide variety of fire-bombings, beatings and death threats.

In a memo that has never before been made public, an FBI investigator captured it simply: The Front, the agent wrote, had "undertaken a campaign to silence all opposition to it."

The scope of the suspected terrorism was extensive. Journalists were slain in Texas, California and Virginia. A string of arsons stretched from Montreal to Orange County, California. Death threats were issued — to individuals, families and businesses across the country. And investigators believed the Front also mailed out communiqués claiming responsibility for the crimes.

Still, some 30 years later, the FBI has arrested no one for the violence or terrorism, much less charged and convicted them. Again and again, local police departments opened investigations that ended with no resolution. The FBI quietly closed its inquiry in the late 1990s, making it one of the most significant unsolved domestic terror cases in the country.

To reconstruct this chapter of history, largely hidden from the majority of Americans, ProPublica and Frontline acquired and scrutinized the FBI's case files, as well as the records of local law enforcement agencies in Houston, San Francisco and the suburbs of Washington, D.C. We tracked down former police detectives, federal agents and prosecutors, and a number of people who had emerged as suspects. We also interviewed former government and military officials from the U.S., Vietnam and Thailand.

As well, we found and spoke with more than two dozen former members of the Front. We tracked down a number of former Front soldiers and traveled to Thailand to meet former Laotian guerillas who had once fought alongside them.

Finally, we spent hours with the families of the dead, and with people who had been shot or beaten. Some of the victims had never spoken publicly — either because they remained afraid or because they had become disillusioned with American law enforcement.

Our investigation lays bare the failure of the authorities to curb the Front's violence and suggests that there are promising leads to pursue should the FBI or others decide to reopen the case. The new information includes accounts from former Front members who had never spoken to law enforcement, one of whom admitted that the Front was responsible for the killing of two of the journalists. Records and interviews show that Minh, as a means of disciplining his ragtag army overseas, ordered the killing of his own recruits, possibly as many as 10. The dead may have included Vietnamese-American citizens of the U.S., giving the FBI authority to investigate the crimes.

ProPublica and Frontline invited the current leadership of the FBI to discuss the bureau's investigation of the Front. James Comey, the bureau's director, would not be interviewed, and neither would the bureau's specialists in domestic terrorism. The FBI also would not answer a series of detailed questions about the actions taken, and not taken, by the bureau during the many years of its investigation. Instead, it issued a statement:

"In the early 1980s, the FBI launched a series of investigations into the alleged politically motivated attacks in Vietnamese-American communities. While initially worked as separate cases across multiple field offices, the investigations were eventually consolidated under a major case designation codenamed 'VOECRN' at the direction of then-Director Louis Freeh. These cases were led by experienced FBI professionals who collected evidence and conducted numerous interviews while working closely with Department of Justice attorneys to identify those responsible for the crimes and seek justice for the victims. Despite those efforts, after 15 years of investigation, DOJ and FBI officials concluded that thus far, there is insufficient evidence to pursue prosecution."

Anh Vo

TABLE OF CONTENTS

Source: ProPublica: FBI summary report on terror crimes.

Spokespeople for the other government agencies with knowledge of the Front's existence would not comment.

Minh ultimately mounted three failed incursions into Vietnam and died in 1987 during one of them. The Front, after a suspected decade of terror stretching from 1980 to

1991, suffered its own divisions and diminished prestige. Some of its onetime leaders have died; others live sprinkled across the country, retired from careers as doctors, restaurant owners or county workers.

Among the former Front members interviewed by ProPublica and Frontline, some insisted the group never engaged in any kind of violent activity in the U.S.

"Never. Never," said Pham To Tu, a Houston resident who said he joined the organization in its early days. The group's enemies, he added, "spread rumors about us."

Every now and again, the Front's former leaders turn out for memorial services or reunions or rallies that still call for the overthrow of the regime in Hanoi. They mingle with men in freshly pressed military uniforms. The air at the events is one of pride and enduring anger, bitterness and defiance.

Trang Q. Nguyen, a co-founder of Little Saigon TV and Radio in Orange County, California, said the Front's efforts to intimidate journalists were well known in the Vietnamese-American media. And she is clear about why she thinks the group was able to elude the authorities: "People were scared."

Like many Vietnamese who fled to the U.S. in the aftermath of the war, Hoang Co Minh experienced a precipitous drop in status when he arrived in this country.

He was an educated man, schooled at Saigon University's law school and the South Vietnamese naval academy, and, later, in the 1960s, at the Naval Postgraduate School in Monterey, California. During the war, he commanded a coastal minesweeper, a 370-ton vessel with a crew of nearly 40 sailors. He held the rank of rear admiral in the South Vietnamese Navy.

Richard Armitage, a former U.S. Navy officer who worked closely with the South Vietnamese Navy before rising to a senior Pentagon position in the 1980s, knew Minh well and called him a "noted combat soldier."

But by 1975, Minh no longer had a country, or a Navy to help direct. He set off for America on the day Saigon fell to the North Vietnamese. By the time he reached the U.S., immigration records show, he had $200 stashed in a Korean bank account, a small chunk of gold, and a couple of cheap rings. He was effectively destitute.

Along with Armitage, Minh had some influential friends: James Kelly, a retired U.S. Navy officer who served as a senior director on the National Security Council during the administrations of Ronald Reagan and George H.W. Bush, invited Minh's family to live with him in the Virginia suburbs outside of Washington. But Minh's new life in America nonetheless started humbly. He did yard work for suburban homeowners and later began hiring himself out as a house painter.

Moving to a foreign land is rarely easy. But the Vietnamese who came to America by the hundreds of thousands during the 1970s weren't the typical economic migrants seeking better jobs and living conditions. They were refugees of a brutal war that had killed an estimated 3 million people. They had been forced to choose between exile or life under the harsh rule of the Communists.

The ensuing exodus was Biblical in scale, set on overloaded boats and in an archipelago of miserable refugee camps, all stuffed with scared people.

Many who stayed in Vietnam wound up dead or in Communist re-education camps where food was scarce and physical abuse abundant. "The Communists had lists of people who had cooperated with the Americans. Those people were called traitors," recalled a South Vietnamese infantryman in "Tears Before the Rain," an oral history. They "were shot right away, right there in the street," he said. "The Communists had no mercy."

Each wave of refugees brought with it disturbing tales of conditions in Southern Vietnam as the Hanoi government remade the country.

By the 1980s, there were some 400,000 Vietnamese living in the U.S., clustering in places like San Francisco, San Jose, Houston, New Orleans, Northern Virginia and Orange County, California. Traumatized, these new communities, often called Little Saigons, proved remarkably resilient, and in time, even wonderfully vibrant. But in the earliest years, they could be insular: handicapped by language barriers, heartsick for their homeland, hungry for vengeance.

Minh recognized the hunger, shared it and set about developing a plan for satisfying it.

After abandoning his house painting business in Virginia, Minh by 1981 had moved to Fresno, California. On immigration paperwork, he said he'd taken up a new job working for a refugee relief organization. Whether he ever did join such an effort, Minh had certainly spent years mixing in circles of fellow former South Vietnamese military officers and others nursing the desire to take up the fight again back in Vietnam. And in those circles, Minh appears to have regained a degree of his former stature.

"I had a very deep respect for him," said Nguyen Xuan Nghia, a former senior Front official. Another former member called Minh "clever" and "brave."

And so when a loose collection of men eager to return to their homeland banded together to form the Front, Minh became their leader. He cultivated a small, devoted following, and within two years he was ready to take his message more broadly to the Vietnamese-American community.

"We resolve to rise up to topple the Viet Cong oligarchy from power," said one early Front propaganda piece. The Front's aim was to create a "humane, free and just democracy."

To do that, interviews and FBI files show, the Front developed a ruthless ethical calculus, believing its men were justified in taking nearly any action to advance their struggle.

Minh had a grand vision for the army he wanted to build. The Front would not only recruit in the U.S., but also use its network of contacts among former South Vietnamese government and military officials to attract volunteer soldiers from the ranks of refugees in Asia and Australia.

In time, Minh secured a tract of land in the forests of Northeast Thailand to establish a secret base of operations. The Front's recruits would live at the base, drilling and strategising. When the moment was right, they would slip into Vietnam and mount a classic guerrilla campaign, linking up with anti-Communist partisans within the country, spreading revolt from village to village. Eventually, the Hanoi government would collapse just as Saigon had.

Like any army, the rebels needed a reliable supply chain that could deliver all the necessities of combat to the base. Weapons. Ammunition. Food. Medicine. Uniforms. Communications gear.

To keep the warriors equipped, Minh and his colleagues created a sophisticated fundraising apparatus in the U.S. It started with Front chapters across the country. Chapter members pledged money to the group, often on a monthly basis. The Front began publishing a magazine called Khang Chien, or Resistance, to spread news of their insurgency and bring in more contributions. They even opened a chain of pho noodle houses to generate revenue.

Combat-hardened veterans flocked to the Front. For South Vietnamese soldiers and sailors, the war had certainly been harrowing, but it also had provided a profound sense of purpose and camaraderie. Now many of these veterans found themselves adrift in America, toiling at menial jobs in an alien land. For them, the idea of reviving the fight held deep emotional appeal.

A journalist who attended some of the Front's rallies in the early 1980s described them as "surreal" events with an ecstatic, near-religious feel.

One of the group's founders, Do Thong Minh, helped sketch out the Front's organisational chart in a recent interview. At the top was Hoang Co Minh, who ran the operation from the Front's encampment in Thailand and communicated with his lieutenants around the world via courier and coded messages. His deputy, a South Vietnamese war hero named Le Hong, also helped direct the Front's trainees in Thailand. Another man oversaw the Front's radio operations, which beamed insurrectionist messages into Vietnam from a transmitter in the Thai base.

In the U.S., an executive committee of roughly 10 people handled fundraising and publicity. Led by an ex-colonel from the South Vietnamese army, the committee established Front chapters in Europe and Canada, as well as *Australia* and Asia.

Source : The front   Terror in Little Saigon - ProPublica

LIFE IN ANOTHER COUNTRY

Our life in Australia begins. It was very hard to leave behind our loving family, however, we had to get out and find an easier way to live our lives, to ensure we had a better chance at living a more happy life and give our children the best possible start in life.

After 3 months we moved out of the Midway Hostel which was an immigrant centre in West Melbourne. We found a 3 bedroom house to rent and then started looking for a job to support our two children who were studying in a catholic school.

My wife got a job in a sewing factory and I got a job in a rubber factory. We saved our money and within 12 months we were able to buy a sewing machine with an over locker so my wife could work from home.

We didn't get paid very much for each garment, sometimes we got paid when they collected the garments and others paid us after two or three weeks and then there were times when people didn't pay at all. They simply collected, never paid and we were unable to find them again.

Our income was very low, however, we needed to pay our rent, school fees for both children and our food, which consisted of chicken that was $1/kg, boiled chicken that was $1.5/kg and every second day we got a full bag of bread from the bakery for $3. It was so difficult to support the expenses we had so I got a second part time job in a factory.

In 1985 we had a great opportunity to set up a small clothing factory business that allowed us to finally get a decent income. We worked very hard and the fruits of our labour allowed us to purchase a house within 12 months of starting our business.

Our third child, a son was born soon (March 1987) after we purchased our house. We are very proud of him as he has grown up to become a fashion designer for a very well-known clothing company.

When the recession hit, our business was affected like many others at the time. The Federal Government at the time cut all the clothing imports from overseas that included TFC Textile, and Footwear. This caused the clothing industry to collapse in Australia and unfortunately we had to close our clothing business.

All the garments we had left was taken to the weekend markets so we could sell them and pay for our food and other expenses. This collapse caused me to take time out and reflect on what we could do to maintain our lifestyle. I decided on going to college where I studied a short course on Timber Flooring, this included installation, sanding and polishing of timber floors.

Once I completed my course we again started a business, this time it was all about timber flooring. We started this business back in the early 1990's and it is still operating today. The business supplies all various types of timber flooring that includes solid timber, parquetry, bamboo, laminate etc. Our services provide our customers with the installation, sanding and polishing of all these types of flooring.

Our family work very hard each and every day with no help from anyone. We are so proud of what we have achieved by coming to live in a country like Australia, where there is freedom and peace. We could not have done this elsewhere, so we take each day with much gratitude and care about our community and how we can give back to them. We understand how important it is to have a helping hand. Our lives would have been much easier had we had the support we are now able to give to people in our community.

Our children have grown up to be very successful and we are truly blessed to have the peace of mind that they are in a good place here in Australia. Our other two children have become successful in their own right, one has a degree in Agricultural Science, while the other in Accounting.

The reason we decided to give back to our community was because when we arrived in Australia we found it very difficult as Vietnamese to settle here in a strange new country. We did not know the language, we had to find a job, it was hard fitting into society, we were discriminated against and then we had the added feelings of nostalgia, excitement and sadness all at the same time.

After 30 April of 1975, there were many refugees arriving in Australia, it got to a stage where there were way too many, it was getting very over-crowded and this group of people took advantage of the favours given to them. This was of concern to the Federal Government and the State of Victoria.

A group of 5 people formed an association to help with assembling the Vietnamese and helping them to integrate into a multicultural society. Unfortunately, they did not have the ability or experience in the field of social security. They were newcomers like us trying to make a difference and create a support group for other newcomers to the country. They did however have basic training skills and got some funding from the Immigration department to help them.

The unfortunate part about this association was that it did not help anyone really, they were not able to help our family at all. We were thankful that the Catholic charities like Saint Vincent De Paul and the parishes in our local area were there to support us initially.

There are many well known Vietnamese/Australian's that have made their new home here in Australia very successful, following is a great article that tells their story:

http://www.academia.edu/9984853/
THE VIETNAMESE REFUGEE EXPERIENCE IN AUSTRALIA

We felt so grateful, yet we did not want others to go through the same problems many Vietnamese of that time endured when first arriving in Australia, so we decided it was time to give back to our people and help them in every way we could.

GIVING BACK TO OUR PEOPLE

There were many Vietnamese that arrived in Melbourne that needed support as many of them had no one or nowhere to go. This is why it was decided that an association should be formed to be able to give back to our people in the way of a support group where they could feel comfortable and safe.

A Vietnamese Association was formed as a Not for Profit organisation. This association's core aim was to provide services to helping all Australian Vietnamese to be able to establish a life in Victoria, Australia. It was to help them with all the basics of living in Australia like:

- How to find accommodation and housing
- How to educate yourself for better employment opportunities
- Social security
- Education for children
- Finances

It was very pleasing to see that there was a group of people willing to help and support people that were new to the country. People that understood what we needed, knowing that support was important for people that were in a strange new country. Remembering that these people came from a country fuelled with terror and fear. So it was a blessing to find an association of people willing to help…or so we thought. It turned out they had not setup their association properly and were not running it to the best interest of their community.

I believe that it was a case of not fully understanding the implications of following the proper procedures and records that need to be kept to make sure that you comply to Australian laws when it comes to running a Not for Profit organisation.

It needs to be noted that there are many people out there that abuse the system by setting up a Not for Profit association under the wrong pretences; instead of helping their local communities, are in it purely for themselves and how they can help their own financial position.

As with all organisations, especially with Not for Profit's, it is their duty of care to show the financials each year to the members of the association. Not all members take an active role in making sure that the board are honest in their roles and complying to the rules and regulations that are required by Australian law for Not for Profit organisations.

In most instances, this is how many of these organisations fall under the radar and get away with running these organisations unlawfully.

It is my duty to the people of Australia as an Australian citizen to make sure that this does not happen again. The experience my family and I endured was not very nice and I would love to share with others through this book how you can avoid the same situation as us.

This is our way of giving back to our people and the people of Australia who have made us feel most welcome and have given us an amazing opportunity by allowing us to be a part of their community.

The following chapters will help you understand what you need to do and where to go to setup a successful Not for Profit organisation.

Anh Vo

CREATING A COMMUNITY

The intention of this chapter is to give you a step-by-step process to help you create your Not for Profit organisation the correct way.

Starting a charity

In this chapter you will find the information about what you'll need to think about if you want to start a new charity or organisation.

Following is a checklist to look at before you start your charity or organisation:

Take some time to do some planning before you go ahead and start a charity – it will help in achieving your goals, as well as identifying possible challenges or risks. This is a list of things you'll need to consider.

Do some background research

Focus on what you want to achieve. Is setting up a new charity the best way to achieve your goals? There may be an existing charity or not-for-profit that already does what you want to do or that may take on your idea as a project that it can support.

You can search the ACNC Register to find registered charities that you could support or work on a project with. There are also other not-for-profit resources you can search for online.

There are benefits (such as the ability to apply for charity tax concessions) that come with registration, but registered charities also have ongoing obligations.

Outline your purpose

Consider and write down in detail what you want to achieve with your charity, and what your timelines are. This helps work out how you may wish to set it up. Ask:

- What will your charity try to achieve?

- What will its main activities be?

- What programs or services will you provide?

- Who is your target audience?

- Who will benefit from the charity's activities and programs?

- Why is there a need for this new charity?

- How long will your charity last? Will it be for a one-off short-term project or an ongoing long-term venture?

If you want to set up a charity, make sure it only has charitable purposes. If you decide to apply to register, the purpose will affect which charity subtypes your organisation can be registered with. Please refer to the ACNC website for more information on this.

Think about the resources required

Consider how much money or other resources your charity is likely to need, in starting up and ongoing costs. It may be worth getting financial and business advice.

- Do you have any money or other resources?

- What assets might you need, such as a physical location, equipment, vehicles?

- What ongoing costs might you have, such as utilities, rent, licences, insurance, salaries?

- How will you raise money?

- Will you require ongoing income?

- Do you need investors?

- Do you need staff or volunteers? How many?

Consider any fundraising requirements

Charities raise money in many different ways, including:

- charging membership fees

- door knocks or other public appeals, including social media and letter campaigns

- highway collections

- events like conferences, movie nights or fun runs

- public auctions

- selling goods.

The ACNC does not regulate fundraising or gaming activities (such as raffles). These activities are regulated by:

- state and territory laws that may require you to get a licence, to report or that set out how you fundraise

- corporations and consumer laws.

Find out more information on fundraising by contacting the state or territory regulator in the state or territory you wish to raise money in. Also be aware of the risks of sending money overseas, and the obligations your charity will have to take appropriate steps to reduce these risks. You can find out more about this in the Attorney-General's Department's Living safely together: guide to help not-for-profits meet Australian obligations.

Understand the importance of legal structure

The legal structure you choose should meet your charity's needs, now and, hopefully, into the future. Charities have a range of structures, incorporated or unincorporated, and there may be more than one that works for your charity. For example, charities can be incorporated under Commonwealth or state laws. Your charity's legal structure will affect many things, such as its legal identity (whether it can be sued), its governance structure (who makes what types of decisions), who is liable for its debts and its specific responsibilities, such as what its reporting or other compliance obligations are.

The ACNC does not register charities according to their legal structure, but you will be asked what your organisation's structure is (also called its 'entity type') if you apply to register with them.

Your decision on legal structure will need to take into account:

- the likely size of your charity, and how complex its activities will be

- whether your charity will have employees or volunteers

- the accountability your charity will have to its members (if any) and the community

- the potential personal liability of members or office holders for things done by them on behalf of the charity

- whether your charity will be applying for government grants

- whether your charity will want to operate in more than one state or territory, or even overseas

- your charity's eligibility for tax concessions.

The advantage of having a formal (incorporated) legal structure is that you can do things such as rent an office, borrow money, apply for government grants or take out insurance in the name of the organisation (rather than, for example, in the name of an individual committee member).

Incorporated structures

The most commonly used incorporated legal structures for charities (and other not-for-profits) include:

- incorporated associations (the most common type) – the name will be something like 'XYZ Incorporated' or 'XYZ Inc'

- companies limited by guarantee (the next most common structure) – for example, 'XYZ Limited' or "XYZ Ltd'

- non-trading co-operatives – the name must include the words 'Cooperative' and 'Limited' or 'Ltd', and

- Indigenous corporations – for example, 'XYZ Aboriginal Corporation'.

Unincorporated structures

If your charity is not incorporated, it could be a trust (for example, 'XYZ Fund', or 'XYZ Foundation') or an unincorporated association (a less formal structure, with no separate legal identity).

Consider getting professional advice

Each structure has advantages and disadvantages – it is important to balance these against your charity's particular circumstances and plans. This is an important decision, so consider getting legal and other professional advice early, and make sure it is specific to your situation. For example, a charity may be able to be incorporated under state law rules for incorporation under a state law may still not meet ACNC requirements to be registered as a charity.

Read the ATO's guidance on different legal structures for not-for-profits.

Explore other legal and regulatory issues

There are many legal implications in setting up a charity, and it may have to comply with a wide range of laws, including Commonwealth, state and territory laws. Consider getting professional (including financial and legal) advice so you can think through your options.

- Where will you operate? Will this be across state or territory borders?
- Will you want to receive charity tax concessions?
- What other legal obligations will apply (such as workplace health and safety laws, employment laws, fundraising laws)?

Decide how your charity will be managed

- Does your charity need a governing body, such as a board or committee, or trustees?
- What kind of governance (rules, practices) will your charity have?
- Will you have formal processes for things like meetings, making or changing

your rules or other decisions?

- Where will you operate from, a dedicated shop front, home office, shared spaced with another organisation?

You can read more about governance in the tools and resources section on the ACNC website. If your charity is registered with the ACNC, it will also need to comply with governance standards.

Plan how to promote your charity and its work

Consider the kind of involvement you would like from the public and potential investors/donors, and how you will communicate its goals and activities.

- How will you promote your charity and encourage people to get involved?
- How will you get information out to your target audience?
- What are your main ways to publicise information?
- Will you need a website or other communication tools?

More information

- Registering with the ACNC (including the benefits of registration, such as being on the ACNC Register and being able to apply for charity tax concessions).
- View the ACNC webinar video: Before you apply to register a charity or sign up for a webinar.
- Information about Commonwealth, state and local regulators your charity may have obligations to.
- Template governing documents that charities can use when they are setting up, or considering changing structure, that can be adapted to suit their particular circumstances.

The ACNC Advice Services team can provide information to help you to apply to register your organisation as a charity and explain its obligations to the ACNC, but they cannot provide legal or other professional advice, such as on legal structure.

Anh Vo

External resources

- ATO: Guidance for non-profits

- Fundraising Institute of Australia (peak body) – see its Principles & Standards of Fundraising Practice

- Community Door (managed by QCOSS with Queensland government funding – with multi-lingual resources about starting an organisation)

- National Pro Bono Resource Centre

- Not-for-profit Law @ Justice Connect (NSW and Victorian site with general information for not-for-profits, including information on getting started)

- Not for Profit Compliance Support Centre (Victorian site with general information)

Links to resources in this chapter:

- Search the ACNC Register - http://www.acnc.gov.au/ACNC/FindCharity/QuickSearch/ACNC/OnlineProcessors/Online_register/Search_the_Register.aspx?noleft=1

- Ongoing Obligations - http://acnc.gov.au/ACNC/Manage/Ongoing_Obs/ACNC/Edu/On_obgtns.aspx?hkey=f93bd0b9-82fe-4e58-84e1-02d57a20c8eb

- Charitable Purposes - http://acnc.gov.au/ACNC/Register_my_charity/Who_can_register/What_char_purp/ACNC/Reg/Charitable_purpose.aspx

- Examples of Charitable Purposes - http://acnc.gov.au/ACNC/Publications/Templates/Example_CharitablePurpose.aspx

- Charity Subtypes - http://www.acnc.gov.au/ACNC/Register_my_charity/Who_can_register/Typ_char/ACNC/Reg/TypesCharPurp.aspx

- State or Territory Regulator - http://acnc.gov.au/ACNC/About_ACNC/Site_information/List_of_regulators/ACNC/Site/Regulator_list.aspx

- Living Safely Together - https://www.livingsafetogether.gov.au/informationadvice/Pages/ConflictinSyria/ConflictinSyrialegalinformationforAustralians.aspx

- Incorporated Associations & Companies Limited by Guarantee - http://www.asic.gov.au/for-business/starting-a-company/how-to-start-a-company/

registering-not-for-profit-or-charitable-organisations/

- Indigenous Corporations - http://www.oric.gov.au/

- Trust - https://www.ato.gov.au/General/Trusts/

- Tools and Resources - http://acnc.gov.au/ACNC/Manage/Tools/ACNC/Edu/Tools/MainTools.aspx

- Registering with the ACNC - http://acnc.gov.au/ACNC/Register_my_charity/ACNC/Reg/Reg_charity.aspx

- Before you apply to register a charity - http://acnc.gov.au/ACNC/Pblctns/Media_centre/Multimedia/ACNC/Comms/Multimedia/Webinar06072015.aspx

- Sign up for a webinar - http://www.acnc.gov.au/ACNC/Manage/Tools/ACNC_webinars/ACNC/Edu/Tools/ACNCwebinars.aspx

- Template Governing Documents - http://www.acnc.gov.au/ACNC/Reg/Template_GovDocStT.aspx

Other Languages

Please visit the link below if you need to look at how all this is done in your own language:

http://www.acnc.gov.au/ACNC/Contact_us/Trans_And_Interpreter/Languages_ACNC/ACNC/Comms/Langs.aspx?noleft=1

© Commonwealth of Australia 2014

Anh Vo

WHO CAN REGISTER FOR A CHARITY ORGANISATION?

Follow this step-by-step process to work out your eligibility:

Who can apply to be registered?

To be eligible to be registered as a charity with the ACNC, your organisation must be able to show that it is a 'charity'. In other words it must:

- be not-for-profit

- have only charitable purposes that are for the public benefit

- be complying with ACNC governance standards

- not have any disqualifying purposes (for example engaging in, or promoting activities that are unlawful or contrary to public policy or promote or oppose a political party or candidate for political office), and

- not be an individual, political party or government entity.

To register, it must also have an Australian Business Number (ABN) with the right 'entity type'.

Follow these steps to work out if your organisation can apply to register.

Step 1: Is my organisation a not-for-profit?

Generally, a not-for-profit is an organisation that does not operate for the profit, personal gain or other benefit of particular people (for example, its members, the people who run it or their friends or relatives). The definition of not-for-profit applies both while the organisation is operating and if it 'winds up' (closes down).

To be registered, your organisation must show the ACNC that it operates on a not-for-profit basis. For many organisations this can be done by showing that:

- their governing documents include suitable not-for-profit clauses, and

- they act consistently with these clauses.

It can still be a not-for-profit if it simply provides a benefit to a member while genuinely carrying out its charitable purpose, or pays a member a reasonable amount for services they have provided or reasonable reimbursements.

A not-for-profit can make a profit, but any profit made must be used for its charitable purpose(s).

Step 2: Does my not-for-profit have a charitable purpose?

A purpose is what your not-for-profit has been set up to achieve or what your activities work toward. Some people also call this your organisation's mission or object.

To be a charity, all of your not-for-profit's purposes must be charitable, except purposes that are 'incidental or ancillary to' (further or aid) the charitable purposes.

The law recognises many kinds of purposes as charitable.

The *Charities Act 2013* (Cth) lists twelve charitable purposes:

- advancing health
- advancing education
- advancing social or public welfare
- advancing religion
- advancing culture
- promoting reconciliation, mutual respect and tolerance between groups of individuals that are in Australia
- promoting or protecting human rights
- advancing the security or safety of Australia or the Australian public
- preventing or relieving the suffering of animals

- advancing the natural environment

- promoting or opposing a change to any matter established by law, policy or practice in the Commonwealth, a state, a territory or another country, (where that change furthers or opposes one or more of the purposes above) and

- other similar purposes 'beneficial to the general public' (a general category).

Other purposes that were recognised as charitable by the general law before the Charities Act came into effect continue to be charitable (for example, the provision of a public facility).

Some examples of not-for-profits with charitable purposes include:

- disability support organisations

- accommodation services for people experiencing homelessness

- non-government schools

- animal welfare agencies.

Subtypes of charity

If the ACNC decide your organisation's purposes are charitable, and that it is otherwise eligible, they can register your charity. When they register it, they register it as a 'subtype' of charity, which reflects its purpose or purposes (for example, as a charity advancing education). The other recognised subtypes are public benevolent institutions and health promotion charities.

You will need to work out what your organisation's charitable purpose is, so you can select the appropriate subtype during the application process. Only choose the subtype or subtypes that apply to your not-for-profit.

Additional tax benefits for some charity subtypes

Extra tax benefits (such as fringe benefits tax exemption or endorsement as a deductible gift recipient (DGR)) are available to a charity that can show it is a:

- charity with a purpose of the advancement of religion - http://

www.acnc.gov.au/ACNC/Pblctns/Factsheets/ACNC/FTS/Fact_RelChar.aspx

- public benevolent institution (PBI), or - http://www.acnc.gov.au/ACNC/Pblctns/Factsheets/ACNC/FTS/Fact_PBI.aspx

- health promotion charity - http://www.acnc.gov.au/ACNC/Pblctns/Factsheets/ACNC/FTS/Fact_HPC.aspx

There are strict requirements that apply and you must be able to demonstrate that your organisation can meet these before it can be registered as being one of these subtypes, for example, by providing supporting information about its activities and expenditure.

Public benevolent institutions (PBIs)

A public benevolent institution is a type of charitable institution whose main purpose is to relieve poverty, sickness, suffering, distress, misfortune, disability or helplessness.

Examples of public benevolent institutions include:

- some hospitals and hospices
- some disability support services
- some aged care services
- providers of low rental or subsidised housing for people in need.

Find out more about public benevolent institutions - http://www.acnc.gov.au/ACNC/Pblctns/Factsheets/FS_PBI/ACNC/FTS/Fact_PBI.aspx

Health promotion charities

A health promotion charity is a charitable institution whose principal activity is to promote the prevention or control of diseases in people. This may include providing public information about a disease, research to develop cures or treatments, or providing equipment to help people who are suffering from the disease. Examples of health promotion charities include:

- some community health care providers

- some medical research organisations

- organisations that work to raise awareness of human diseases.

Find out more about health promotion charities - http://www.acnc.gov.au/ACNC/Pblctns/Factsheets/ACNC/FTS/Fact_HPC.aspx

Even if your organisation is not eligible to be registered as a public benevolent institution or a health promotion charity, it may still be able to register as a charity.

Deductible gift recipients (DGRs)

Certain DGR categories require charities to be registered with the ACNC before applying for DGR status with the ATO. If your organisation is a charity that wants to apply for DGR status, you may need to be registered with the ACNC first.

You can apply to register as a charity with the ACNC and apply for deductible gift recipient (DGR) status with the ATO at the same time.

Step 3: Does my not-for-profit benefit the public?

Your not-for-profit's charitable purpose must be for the public benefit.

There are many ways it can benefit the public – it can provide goods, services, education, counselling or spiritual guidance, or improve the environment. Some types of purposes (for example, advancing education, relieving poverty, advancing religion) are also presumed to be for the public benefit, unless there is evidence otherwise.

Charities may aim to benefit the public generally, or a particular group of people (for example, a local community, refugees or young people). Charities do not have to benefit everyone in a community, but any restrictions must be consistent with their charitable purpose. For example, a food bank could restrict its beneficiaries to people who cannot afford their own food, but it could not restrict it to people based on their appearance.

Your organisation may not be a charity if it is too restrictive in who can receive benefits. For example, an organisation set up to provide scholarships to employees of a particular employer is unlikely to be a charity.

Find out more about public benefit - http://www.acnc.gov.au/ACNC/ Register_my_charity/Who_can_register/Public_benefit/ACNC/Reg/ Public_benefit.aspx

You will be asked to state who will benefit from your not-for-profit's activities (its beneficiaries) as part of the application process.

Step 4: Does my not-for-profit fit the other rules for registration?

As well as needing to fit the legal definition of charity, to be eligible to register your not-for-profit must:

- have an Australian Business Number (ABN)

- meet the governance standards, and - http://www.acnc.gov.au/ACNC/ Manage/Governance/ACNC/Edu/GovStds_overview.aspx

- not be a type of organisation that cannot be registered.

Organisations that cannot be registered

Your organisation cannot be registered as a charity if it is:

- a political party

- a 'government entity' — this is part of an Australian or foreign government or one of its agencies, and some organisations established by a state or territory under a law, or

- included in a written decision made by an Australian government agency or judge that lists it as engaging in or supporting terrorist or other criminal activities.

Also, the ACNC cannot register an individual, or a partnership (a particular legal structure) as a charity.

Legal Meaning of Charity

'Charity' has a technical legal meaning. When the ACNC makes decisions about whether to register your organisation as a charity, they apply the law:

- made by judges ('common law') on the meaning of charity and charitable purposes
- taking account of relevant legislation such as the ACNC Act, Charities Act 2013 (Cth) (Charities Act) and Charities (Consequential Amendments and Transitional Provisions) Act 2013 (Cth) (the Charities Consequential and Transitional Act)

The Australian Taxation Office (ATO) has produced tax rulings on charitable status, which set out the ATO Commissioner's opinion about the way the tax law will be interpreted and applied. Taxation Ruling (TR) 2011/4 sets out how the ATO interprets the meaning of charity. This and other ATO rulings are not binding on the ACNC. However, they will have regard to what was previously considered by the ATO to be a charity, including what is set out in taxation rulings.

ACNC Commissioner Interpretation Statements

The ACNC are publishing ACNC Commissioner's Interpretation Statements as they are developed. These set out the approach they will take to interpreting the law on registration of charities.

These statements will progressively replace the ATO's tax rulings.

Read the Commissioner's Interpretation Statements - http://www.acnc.gov.au/ACNC/Pblctns/Interp/ACNC/Publications/InterpStmt.aspx

Charities Act – the statutory definition of charity

The Commonwealth Parliament passed the *Charities Act 2013* (Cth) (the Charities Act) and the Charities (Consequential Amendments and Transitional Provisions) Act 2013 (Cth) (the Charities Consequential and Transitional Act) on 27 June and they came into effect on 1 January 2014. The Charities Act clearly sets out the legal meaning of charity. The ACNC must apply this law.

The Charities Act restates the existing (judge-made) law in modern language and also recognises charitable purposes such as the protection of human rights, the promotion of reconciliation and tolerance, and by recognising that many modern charities advance causes by preventing, educating, researching and raising awareness. The Charities Consequential and Transitional Act supports us to administer the Charities Act. For example, it contains a table that sets out how the previous table of ACNC charity subtypes match up with the new list of charity subtypes.

Find out more in the Charities Act, the Charities Consequential and Transitional Act - http://www.acnc.gov.au/ACNC/About_ACNC/ACNC_leg/ACNC/Legal/ ACNC_leg.aspx

and the Explanatory Memorandum - http://www.aph.gov.au/Parliamentary_Business/ Bills_Legislation/Bills_Search_Results/Result?bId=r5077

and the background to the Act - http://www.treasury.gov.au/ ConsultationsandReviews/Consultations/2013/A-statutory-definition-of-charity

Effect on existing registered charities

Generally, the Charities Act will have no impact on existing registered charities, and the ACNC expect that most charities will not have to do anything like changing their purposes once the Act has commenced. In particular, there has been no change to the existing areas of the law like advocacy, the definition of religion, or the commercial activity of charities.

In a few cases (for example, native title bodies, government bodies, disaster relief funds), the Charities Act clarifies some difficult areas of law.

Over time, the ACNC will work with charities to transfer them to the new subtypes created by the Charities Act, if these apply to them. There will be a period of 18 months for this to happen.

Charities applying for registration with the ACNC

The ACNC uses the definition of charity set out in the Charities Act (which came into effect on 1 January 2014) when making decisions on registration applications.

If a registration application was received before 1 January 2014, the law that is used will depend on when the registration decision is made. If it is made after 1 January 2014, the ACNC will apply the definition of charity in the Charities Act 2013. A new registration form became available in January 2014.

As there will only be a few changes to the law as a result of the Charities Act, the ACNC expects that most applications will be decided in the same way as they would have before 1 January 2014.

Changes from the Charities Act

The Charities Act clarifies that to be a recognised as a charity, an organisation must:

- be not-for-profit
- have only charitable purposes that are for the public benefit
- not have a disqualifying purpose
- not be an individual, a political party or a government entity.

Charitable purpose

The Charities Act confirms that an organisation must only have charitable purposes. It can have other purposes, but these must only be incidental or ancillary purposes that further or assist the charitable purpose or purposes. Read more about charitable purposes and charity subtypes.

Public benefit

The Charities Act does not change the meaning of public benefit. The new definition maintains that certain purposes (for example, advancing education or religion, relieving poverty) are, in the absence of evidence to the contrary, for the public benefit. The Charities Act does not change the way the ACNC determines public benefit in other cases.

Advocacy

The Charities Act makes clearer the existing law on advocacy and political activity by charities. A charity can advance its charitable purposes in the following ways:

- involving itself in public debate on matters of public policy or public administration through, for example, research, hosting seminars, writing opinion pieces, interviews with the media

- supporting, opposing, endorsing and assisting a political party or candidate because this would advance the purposes of the charity (for example, a human rights charity could endorse a party on the basis that the charity considers that the party's policies best promote human rights), and

- giving money to a political party or candidate because this would further the charity's purposes.

There are some things to watch out for:

- charities should check their governing documents (such as a constitution, rules or trust deed) and contracts to make sure that there is nothing that prevents them from advocating

- while a charity can support a political party or candidate, this support must be a way of achieving its purposes rather than a goal in itself (for example, it can't have a hidden purpose of fundraising for a political party)

- if a charity gives money or spends money to support or oppose a political party or candidate, it may need to disclose this under electoral laws (for the Commonwealth rules on this, see the Australian Electoral Commission's guidance) - http://aec.gov.au/Parties_and_Representatives/ financial_disclosure/guides/third-parties/index.htm

Definition of 'Not For Profit'

What is a not-for-profit?

Generally, a not-for-profit is an organisation that does not operate for the profit, personal gain or other benefit of particular people (for example, its members, the people who run it or their friends or relatives). The definition of not-for-profit applies both while the organisation is operating and if it 'winds up' (closes down).

Benefits to members

It can still be a not-for-profit if it simply provides a benefit to a member while genuinely carrying out its purpose. For example, organisations such as self-help groups can be not-for-profits if the benefits provided to members are consistent with the purposes of the organisation. So, a self-help group for young disadvantaged parents can provide counselling services to a young parent who is a member of the organisation. The member is also a person in need who is helped by the organisation.

Types of benefits

A not-for-profit can provide direct benefits (such as distributing money or gifts) or indirect benefits (such as a member receiving help that is consistent with the not-for-profits' purpose).

A staff member and, sometimes, a responsible person (such as a board or committee member or trustee) can be paid for their work, but not an unreasonable amount. Your organisation's governing documents (such as its constitution) may include clauses about reasonable payments and benefits.

Making a profit

A not-for-profit can make a profit, but any profit made must be used for its purpose(s). It can keep profits as long as there is a genuine reason for this and it is to do with its purpose. For example, a good reason to keep profits may be to save up for starting a new project, building new infrastructure or accumulating a reserve so it continues to be sustainable.

If an organisation continues to hold onto significant profits indefinitely, without using them for its charitable purpose, this may suggest that the organisation is not working solely towards its stated charitable purpose (and is not operating as a not-for-profit).

Demonstrating not-for-profit character

To be registered with the ACNC, you need to show that your organisation meets the requirement of being a not-for-profit. You can do this by having particular statements (clauses) in your organisation's governing documents, and following these. Sample clauses may include wording as used in the following examples.

The not-for-profit clause

This clause sets out how the organisation's assets and income are to be used and distributed.

'The assets and income of the organisation shall be applied solely to further its objects and no portion shall be distributed directly or indirectly to the members of the organisation except as genuine compensation for services rendered or expenses incurred on behalf of the organisation.'

The dissolution clause

This clause sets out what happens to the organisation's assets if it dissolves or winds up (closes down). To satisfy the ACNC requirements of being a charity, the clause must require the assets to go to another charity.

'In the event of the organisation being dissolved, all assets that remain after such dissolution and the satisfaction of all debts and liabilities shall be transferred to another organisation with similar purposes, which is charitable at law and which has rules prohibiting the distribution of its assets and income to its members.'

Anh Vo

The DGR revocation clause

This clause is used if the organisation has applied for deductible gift recipient status.

'If the organisation is wound up or its endorsement as a deductible gift recipient is revoked (whichever occurs first), any surplus of the following assets shall be transferred to another organisation with similar objects, which is charitable at law, to which income tax deductible gifts can be made:
a. gifts of money or property for the principal purpose of the organisation
b. contributions made in relation to an eligible fundraising event held for the principal purpose of the organisation
c. money received by the organisation because of such gifts and contributions.'

Legal structure

We also accept that some organisations can show their not-for-profit character through the operation of certain laws, such as state or territory incorporated associations legislation and trust law (for example, charitable trusts).

Requirement to only have charitable purposes that are not disqualifying purposes

To be registered as a charity, your organisation must have a charitable purpose or purposes.

What is your organisation's 'purpose'?

Your organisation's 'purpose' is what your organisation has been set up to achieve. Some people also refer to this as your organisation's mission.

How the ACNC decide if your purposes are charitable

When you apply to register your organisation as a charity, you need to demonstrate its charitable purpose. Generally, the ACNC will decide what your organisation's purposes are by looking at:

- your organisation's governing documents (for example, its constitution, rules or deed) – these usually set out its purpose or 'objects'

- other types of evidence, such as your organisation's activities, annual reports, financial statements and corporate documents.

Some activities may not seem to be charitable, but are appropriate if they are to further a charitable purpose. For example, your organisation may have activities designed to raise money so it can pursue its charitable purposes.

Example: An organisation that provides accommodation for homeless youth operates a recycled clothing shop, where the profits raised are used to provide this accommodation.

What happens after the ACNC decide your purposes are charitable

Once they decide your organisation's purposes are charitable, and that it is otherwise eligible, they register your charity. When they register it, they register it as a 'subtype' of charity, which reflects its purpose or purposes (for example, as a charity advancing education).

The subtype or subtypes of charity they register your charity as can affect the tax concessions that may be available to it. You may be required to provide further information to support an application for particular subtypes of charity, such as a public benevolent institution or health promotion charity.

What they recognise as charitable purposes

'Charitable purpose' has a special legal meaning, developed over the years by the courts and parliament. The courts have recognised many different charitable purposes, and as society changes new charitable purposes are accepted.

The *Charities Act 2013* (Cth) lists twelve charitable purposes:

- advancing health

- advancing education

- advancing social or public welfare

- advancing religion

- advancing culture

- promoting reconciliation, mutual respect and tolerance between groups of individuals that are in Australia

- promoting or protecting human rights

- advancing the security or safety of Australia or the Australian public

- preventing or relieving the suffering of animals

- advancing the natural environment

- promoting or opposing a change to any matter established by law, policy or practice in the Commonwealth, a state, a territory or another country (where that change furthers or opposes one or more of the purposes above), and

- other similar purposes 'beneficial to the general public' (a general category).

Purposes that the law recognised as charitable before the Charities Act came into effect will continue to be charitable. The charity subtypes of public benevolent institution and health promotion charity also continue to be recognised.

Charities can have more than one charitable purpose

Your organisation may have more than one charitable purpose. For example, your organisation may educate the public about the environment, and so advance education as well as the environment.

The law requires **all** of your organisation's purposes to be charitable, except for purposes that are 'incidental or ancillary to' (further or aid) the charitable purposes.

Your organisation may have more than one purpose, and many activities, and still be a charity, as long as these all further the charitable purpose.

Please Note: If your organisation has non-charitable purposes and these do not further its charitable purposes, your organisation is unlikely to be registered as a charity.

Some purposes are not recognised as charitable

Some purposes may benefit the community, but not fit the legal meaning of charitable purpose. For example, your organisation may not fit the legal meaning of charity if it is a:

- **social club** – unless its main purpose is charitable such as to help people who are socially isolated or disadvantaged, and the club's social activities are the way it achieves this purpose

- **sporting and recreational organisation** – unless its main purpose is charitable such as providing sporting activities for the people with disabilities or the elderly

- **professional or trade group** – unless its main purpose is charitable, such as advancing education.

These organisations may still:

- be not-for-profits and exempt from income tax, or

- qualify as charities under state or territory laws.

However, they are unlikely to fall within the general legal meaning of charity as the ACNC apply it.

Some purposes cannot be charitable

Some purposes are deliberately disqualified from being charitable, such as the purposes of:

- engaging in or promoting activities that are unlawful or against public policy, or

- promoting or opposing a political party or a candidate for political office.

Unlawful activities

Unlawful activities would include being engaged in tax evasion, people or drug trafficking, dealing in weapons or illegal goods. In some cases, a charity may be set up for charitable purposes but be used to hide or transfer money that has been gained illegally.

In these cases, the organisation is not a charity because its activities show that its **true** purpose is to engage in unlawful activities.

Activities that are against public policy

It is not against public policy to have a purpose of advocating for a change in government policy or law, or from promoting a law or policy – in certain situations these may be charitable purposes, for example advancing public debate on a charitable topic.

An example of an activity against public policy would be educating people in how to build illegal weapons. Even though education is a charitable purpose, it would not be a charitable purpose to educate people in a way that may put members of the public at risk.

Purpose of promoting or opposing a political party or candidate

An organisation that has a purpose of promoting or opposing a political party or candidate for political office cannot be a charity. For example, an organisation that exists to fundraise for the election of a political candidate is not a charity.

Charities can engage in some policy debate

Charities can still distribute information or engage in debate about the policies of political parties or candidates, where these activities must be ways of achieving their charitable purposes.

Purposes that are for the public benefit

To be registered as a charity, a not-for profit must have charitable purposes that 'is for the public benefit'.

Benefit must be to the public

A charity's purpose is for the public benefit if achieving this purpose would be of benefit to the public generally or a sufficient section of the public.

A sufficient section of the community may be, for example, a local community, followers of a particular religion, people with a particular disability, refugees or young people.

Types of benefit

There are many ways a charity's purpose can benefit the public, for example, it can provide goods, services, education, counselling or spiritual guidance, or improve the environment.

Restrictive membership can still benefit the public

Restriction related to purpose

A charity may restrict its benefits to a particular class or group of people if the class is not closed, and the restriction advances its charitable purpose. For example, an organisation whose purpose is to provide assistance services to refugees can still be a charity if its services are available to all refugees (so the class is not closed) as the restriction advances its charitable purpose.

However, an organisation may not be a charity if it is too restrictive in who can receive benefits. For example, an organisation set up to provide scholarships to employees of a particular employer is unlikely to be a charity as it is a closed class of beneficiaries who are linked by ties to a single individual or company.

Restriction to manage services

A charity can also limit access to manage its services. For example, a school may require students to enrol, legal clinics may accept only certain types of cases, and libraries may impose borrowing rules.

When public benefit test is limited or does not apply

Traditional Indigenous land rights

The Charities Act makes it clear that organisations that receive, hold or manage benefits relating to native title or traditional Indigenous land rights are for the public benefit even though they may benefit people who are related to each other. This is a complex area of law.

Relief of necessitous circumstances

For organisations relieving the necessitous circumstances of Australian individuals (people in need), the benefit does not have to be directed to the general public.

Closed religious orders and self-help groups

The public benefit test does **not** apply for:

- closed or contemplative religious orders that regularly pray on request from members of the general public, and
- self-help groups that have an open and non-discriminatory membership and were established to help people affected by a particular disadvantage or discrimination, or unmet need, by people affected by that disadvantage or discrimination or need.

Complying with ACNC Governance Standards

Charities must meet a set of governance standards to be registered and remain registered with the ACNC. The governance standards do not apply to a limited class of charities called 'basic religious charities' - http://www.acnc.gov.au/ACNC/Manage/ManageType/Basic_rel_ent/ACNC/Edu/Basic_rel_char.aspx

Charities do not need to submit anything to the ACNC to show they meet the standards, but must have evidence of meeting the standards that they can provide if requested.

What are governance standards?

The governance standards are a set of core, minimum standards that deal with how charities are run (including their processes, activities and relationships) – their governance.

The standards require charities to remain charitable, operate lawfully, and be run in an accountable and responsible way. They help charities remain trusted by the public and continue to do their charitable work. Because the governance standards are a set of high-level principles, not precise rules, your charity must decide how it will comply with them.

Your charity must be able to demonstrate that the steps it has taken to comply are appropriate for it (considering factors such as its size, purpose and activities). For example, a larger charity or one with vulnerable beneficiaries may need to take extra steps to comply with the standards.

What the standards require

Standard 1: Purposes and not-for-profit nature

Charities must be not-for-profit and work towards their charitable purpose. They must be able to demonstrate this and provide information about their purposes to the public.

Standard 2: Accountability to members

Charities that have members must take reasonable steps to be accountable to their members and provide them with adequate opportunity to raise concerns about how the charity is governed.

Standard 3: Compliance with Australian laws

Charities must not commit a serious offence (such as fraud) under any Australian law or breach a law that may result in a penalty of 60 penalty units (currently $10 200) or more.

Standard 4: Suitability of responsible persons

Charities must take reasonable steps to:

- be satisfied that its responsible persons (such as board or committee members or trustees) are not disqualified from managing a corporation under the *Corporations Act 2001 (Cth)* or disqualified from being a responsible person of a registered charity by the ACNC Commissioner, and

- remove any responsible person who does not meet these requirements.

Standard 5: Duties of responsible persons

Charities must take reasonable steps to make sure that responsible persons are subject to, understand and carry out the duties set out in this standard.

How the ACNC will assess compliance

The ACNC expects most charities will already be meeting the governance standards and they focus on charities that have seriously or deliberately breached the governance standards by (for example):

- diverting money to non-charitable purposes

- not disclosing serious conflicts of interest, or

- being grossly negligent with their finances.

The ACNC will act, according to their regulatory approach, (http://www.acnc.gov.au/ACNC/About_ACNC/Regulatory_app/ACNC/Regulatory/Reg_approach.aspx) if they have information that indicates that there may be serious risks involved.

Other rules about registration

There are specific rules about which organisations the ACNC can register. To be eligible to register, your organisation must:

- be a charity (as described above), meaning it is a not-for-profit, has a charitable purpose and is for the public benefit

- have an Australian Business Number (ABN)

- comply with governance standards

- not be a type of organisation that **cannot** be registered.

Your organisation cannot be registered as a charity if it is:

- a political party

- a 'government entity' — this is part of an Australian or foreign government or one of its agencies, and some organisations established under a state or territory law

Anh Vo

- included in a written decision made by an Australian government agency or judge that lists it as engaging in or supporting terrorist or other criminal activities.

Also, the ACNC cannot register an individual, or a partnership (a particular legal structure) as a charity.

If you think your organisation is eligible, you can now apply to register. (https://www.acnc.gov.au/ACNC/Register_my_charity/Start_reg/ACNC/Reg/Apply_to_register.aspx) There is a checklist of things to consider before you start, as well as a guide to the application form, to help you through the process.

Successfully Changing Lives by Building a Community

THE BENEFITS OF REGISTERING FOR A CHARITY ORGANISATION

What are the benefits of ACNC Registration?

Charities must register with the Australian Charities and Not-for-profits Commission (ACNC) before they can receive **charity tax concessions** from the Australian Taxation Office (ATO). If you decide to also apply for tax concessions, you can do this within one form – the ACNC registration application form. Your application for tax concessions will be sent to the ATO, who will decide your organisation's eligibility for tax concessions.

Benefits of registration

Access to charity tax concessions and other benefits
Benefits of registering include being able to:

- apply for charity tax concessions as a charity (such as income tax exemption or goods and services tax concessions) from the ATO (your charity **must** be registered before you can apply for concessions).

- apply for additional tax benefits as a public benevolent institution (PBI), health promotion charity (HPC) or charity for the advancement of religion

- apply for certain categories of deductible gift recipient (DGR) status. Some categories of deductible gift recipient (DGR) status are **only** available to registered charities. If your organisation is a charity that wants to apply for DGR status, you will need to be registered with the ACNC first. If your charity is already a DGR, check the ACNC Register to see if it has automatically been registered with them.

- receive a range of other concessions, benefits or exemptions available to charities under Commonwealth law.

Links to more information:

- Charity tax concessions - http://www.acnc.gov.au/ACNC/Pblctns/Factsheets/ACNC/FTS/Fact_ConcAvail.aspx

- Public benevolent institution (PBI) - http://www.acnc.gov.au/ACNC/Pblctns/Factsheets/FS_PBI/ACNC/FTS/Fact_PBI.aspx

- Health promotion charity (HPC) - http://www.acnc.gov.au/ACNC/Pblctns/ Factsheets/FS_HPC/ACNC/FTS/Fact_HPC.aspx

- Advancement of religion - http://www.acnc.gov.au/ACNC/Pblctns/Factsheets/ ACNC/FTS/Fact_RelChar.aspx

- Certain categories of deductible gift recipient (DGR) status - http:// www.acnc.gov.au/ACNC/Pblctns/Factsheets/ACNC/FTS/Fact_DGR.aspx

- If your charity is already a DGR - http://www.acnc.gov.au/ACNC/FindCharity/ QuickSearch/ACNC/OnlineProcessors/Online_register/ Search_the_Register.aspx?noleft=1

- Other concessions, benefits or exemptions - http://www.acnc.gov.au/ACNC/ Pblctns/Factsheets/ACNC/FTS/Fact_CthBenAvail.aspx

Publicly confirming registration by the national regulator

Registered charities can use the following wording on public documents (such as letterhead, emails and a website) to demonstrate to the public and others your charity's registration with the ACNC:

- [insert charity name] is registered as a charity with the Australian Charities and Not-for-profits Commission ABN [insert 11 digit ABN]. (Please note that a registered charity cannot use the ACNC logo)

Registered charities automatically have a free online presence on the ACNC Register where the public, potential donors and funding agencies can find out information about them.

Additional benefits for some types of charities

Recipients of Commonwealth grants

For recipients of Commonwealth grants, (from 1 June 2013) your grant department is not able to ask you to provide the same information you have provided to the ACNC. Also, if you provide an audited financial statement to the ACNC, then a financial acquittal should not be required, unless the granting activity is higher risk.

Charitable companies limited by guarantee

If your company limited by guarantee is registered with ASIC and also registered with the ACNC:

- you no longer have to pay ASIC filing fees, including the annual review fee

- reporting to the ACNC instead of ASIC (once ACNC financial reporting obligations start, from the 2013–2014 reporting period onwards) means more generous reporting size thresholds. The ACNC thresholds are based on revenue alone and disregard consideration of DGR status. For example, a charity with $245 000 in annual revenue and DGR status would be considered medium under the *Corporations Act 2001 (Cth)* (and would need to have an audit or review), but would be considered small under the ACNC Act (and would not require an audit or review, as they are exempt from providing financial reports)

- charities registered with the ACNC are not required to prepare a directors' report. This may reduce the cost of an audit of a charity, as the auditor is no longer required to review the directors' report to check for inconsistencies with the audited financial report.

Future benefits

Reducing the regulatory burden on charities

The ACNC is working with a range of government agencies and stakeholders on the major task of reducing red tape for charities over time, including by aligning regulatory requirements through working closely with other Commonwealth and state and territory departments and agencies.

The Government of South Australia and the Australian Capital Territory Government have both announced they will move to reduce regulatory duplication in their incorporated associations and charitable collections legislation.

Read more about red tape reduction - http://www.acnc.gov.au/ACNC/About_ACNC/ Redtape_redu/ACNC/Report/Red_tape.aspx

Anh Vo

Gathering charity data and promoting sector research

As well as regulating charities, promoting good governance and compliance, the ACNC is gathering a large amount of data about the nature and activities of charities. This will not only be available on the ACNC Register to raise transparency and accountability, it will also feed into research and policy development in the not-for-profit sector.

Successfully Changing Lives by Building a Community

PREPARING FOR REGISTRATION OF YOUR CHARITY ORGANISATION

Understand the registration and legal structure

Registration Checklist

To complete the registration application form you will need to have the following information about your organisation ready. Use this checklist with the ACNC registration application guide.

Australian Business Number (ABN)

Your organisation needs an ABN to register with the ACNC.
If it doesn't have an ABN, you can apply for an ABN online - https://abr.gov.au/

If your organisation has used its ABN to apply for registration before or had its registration with this ABN revoked, you will need to contact the ACNC via this link (http://www.acnc.gov.au/ACNC/Contact_us/How_to_contact_the_ACNC/ACNC/Adv/ HowToContact.aspx) before you start the application.

If your organisation's ABN hasn't been used to register with them before, and is available, use ABN Lookup (http://www.abr.business.gov.au/) to check that its details on the Australian Business Register (ABR) are correct.

In particular, see if the ABN entry includes your organisation's correct **legal name** and **entity type**. If your ABN has the wrong legal name or a type that cannot be registered, you will need to apply to change your record on the ABR. In some cases, you may need to apply for a new ABN. Visit ABR Help and find out how to change your ABN details (https://abr.gov.au/).

Charity name

This is the formal name as it appears on legal or other official documents. It may need to include certain words by law. For example:

- organisations which are incorporated under state or territory incorporated associations law need to have the word 'Incorporated' or 'Inc' as the last word of their names
- many companies must have the word 'Ltd' at the end of their names

(although, companies can apply to ASIC to have this word removed).

The name of the organisation that is listed on the ABR (legal name) needs to match its charity name (as recorded on its ABN registration). This is the charity name that will be published on the ACNC Register.

Legal structure

You will be asked to describe your organisation's legal structure (as set out in its governing documents) in the application form. There are different types of legal structure. The table below sets out the different structures of organisations that can apply to be registered as charities and the correct ABR type for each legal structure. There are other structures which may be able to be registered.

Legal structure of applicant	Correct ABR type
ACT incorporated association NSW incorporated association NT incorporated association QLD incorporated association SA incorporated association TAS incorporated association VIC incorporated association WA incorporated association Organisation incorporated under legislation	Other Incorporated Entity
Trust (including testamentary trust created in a Will)	Discretionary Investment Trust **OR** Fixed Trust (depending on structure of trust)
Australian Public Company (does not have Pty in its name)	Australian Public Company
Australian Private Company (has Pty in its name)	Australian Private Company
Unincorporated Association	Other Unincorporated Entity
Co-operative	Co-operative

Contact details

Including address for service (email and/or postal), business address and operating locations.

Form contact person details

This is the person we should talk to during the registration process.

Charitable purpose

The purpose or purposes of your organisation. You will also need information about its main:

- activities, and
- beneficiaries.

Financial information

Including main sources of funding. For the current and previous reporting periods.

Responsible person details

Such as directors, trustees or committee members. These people have responsibilities to your organisation, and once registered, to the ACNC.

You will need to provide their:

- name and any previous names
- date of birth
- address and phone numbers
- position within the organisation.

Only their names and positions will be published on the ACNC Register. The other information can be used by the ACNC for proof of identity purposes, so that the ACNC can ensure it only communicates with properly authorised people once your organisation is registered.

You must provide these details for each responsible person in your organisation. The number of responsible persons you have may be included in your governing document (for example, a rule about the number of people necessary for the organisation's management committee).

Governing document or documents (such as a constitution, rules or trust deeds)

These need to:

- show that your organisation is not-for-profit
- be in electronic format, if possible, so you can upload them as part of the application form.

Find out more about:

- showing your organisation is not-for-profit, and
- how to identify your governing documents and provide them to the ACNC. There are other options if your documents are not in electronic format.

Details for applying for charity tax concessions

This is part of the same application form.

If you are requesting one of the following, you will need to understand the Australian Taxation Office (ATO) requirements, and attach any applicable schedules:

- deductible gift recipient (DGR) status
- registration as a public benevolent institution (PBI), or
- registration as a health promotion charity.

Find out more about not-for-profit tax concessions and endorsement requirements in the ATO's guidance for non-profits. (https://www.ato.gov.au/non-profit/) You can apply for ACNC registration first and tax concessions later.

Print out the ACNC Registration Application Guide from the Website.

Using the online form

The form will lead you through the information you need to provide. There are pop-up boxes explaining each step – check your security settings to allow these.

Username and password

Choose a username and password to create your account within the registration system. **This is just for the registration application. You will be provided with a different login for the Charity Portal if your charity is successfully registered.**

The username can be anything you like, but it needs to be unique. They do not recommend that you use your email address. The password needs to be a minimum of nine (9) characters. Make a note of your registration username and password and keep them safe.

If the form does not load, please try refreshing your browser.

Saving incomplete applications

You can save your partially completed application and return to it later if you need to. You can resume your application at any time by navigating to the 'Resume my application' page under the 'Register my charity' tab.

What to expect after applying

After you submit the registration application you will receive an email with a submission number. Have this number and your ABN ready if you need to contact them so they can quickly find your application details.

Every application is allocated to an ACNC case officer. This person will contact you to confirm that your application has been received and to clarify any information if required. If you do not receive the confirmation email or a follow-up phone call, please contact them.

If you decide not to continue with registration please contact the ACNC.

Timeframe for registration

They generally process applications within 28 days if no further information is required.

They will also contact you if any information needs to be clarified. Where needed, they will provide you with advice to ensure your application is processed as quickly as possible.

Successful applicants

Charity pack

They will write to tell you if your application has been successful and send you a charity pack. In the charity pack you will receive:

- a registration letter

- a registration certificate

- a password to log in to the ACNC Charity Portal (https://charity.acnc.gov.au/ ACNCPortal/Charity/Sign_In.aspx? WebsiteKey=15ae55d1-4f4a-4d80-9549-6ea9d089c234&returnurl=%2f)

- information about being a registered charity, including its ongoing obligations (https://www.acnc.gov.au/ACNC/Manage/Ongoing_Obs/ACNC/Edu/ On_obgtns.aspx)

Your charity's Australian Business Number (ABN) will be the unique identifier for ACNC registration and you can use the ABN to search for your charity's entry on the ACNC Register.

Once registered, you can use the following wording on public documents (such as letterhead, emails and a website) to demonstrate to the public and others your charity's registration with the ACNC:

- [insert charity name] is registered as a charity with the Australian Charities and Not-for-profits Commission ABN [insert 11 digit ABN].

Please note that a registered charity cannot use the ACNC logo.

Once your charity is registered, you will be able to use your portal login to make changes to your charity's details, report to them and print a copy of your registration certificate.

Charity tax concessions

If you applied for charity tax concessions (including deductible gift recipient (DGR) status in your registration application), they will forward your charity's information and this part of the application form to the Australian Tax Office (ATO).

The ATO decides if your organisation is entitled to charity tax concessions and/or DGR status. They will notify you of their decision or if you need to provide more information. You can also apply for tax concessions separately if you want to apply for registration first and tax concessions later.

Unsuccessful applicants

They will write to tell you if your application is not successful and why they have come to their decision. You can ask for their decision to be reviewed.

Registration FAQs

What if I've forgotten my login details or can't log in?

If you forget your login username or password, select 'resume my application' from the 'Register my charity' menu tab. From there you can select either the 'forgot my username' or 'forgot my password' options.

What if my organisation's ABN appears to be taken?

If you enter your Australian Business Number (ABN) into the ABN availability screen and the system reports that the ABN you entered is in use, you can:

- re-enter your ABN again, checking that the number is correct
- check the ACNC Register to see which organisation has registered using that ABN.

Please remember that the ACNC does not manage the Australian Business Register.

What will be the date of registration?

The ACNC decides your charity's date of registration. Generally, this will be the date your application for registration was approved by them, but if you want an earlier date let them know when you apply. It must have been eligible for registration on that date.

The earliest date of registration your charity can apply for is 3 December 2012, when the ACNC was established.

What happens to the information I provide about my charity?

Information about your charity will be published on the public ACNC Register (except the dates of birth or residential addresses of any responsible person).

In limited circumstances we may withhold (exclude) your charity's information from the Register if you apply to withhold information.

The ACNC is committed to protecting confidential and sensitive charity information.

Registration Case Study

Happy Helpers (SA)

The Happy Helpers (the Helpers) is a small organisation set up in 2010 to run a homework club in Parkton in Adelaide, South Australia.

How it began and why

The organisation was originally set up by a group of four volunteers who felt that more out-of-school educational support was needed for young people aged 12–18, especially those at risk of disengagement.

The four volunteers called themselves 'the committee'. They are:

- Kara Moon   (a retired police officer)
- Daniel Moon (a small business owner)
- Burak Atalay (a plumber), and

- Jill Chan   (a teacher).

How it has developed

The Helpers began by operating a homework club at a local school in Parkton. Members of the committee worked in pairs to run a session three times a week. Parents at the school were grateful for their work and some volunteered to fill extra shifts with the club. This provided the committee with an opportunity to work on developing resources and coordinating a roster of volunteers. The Helpers also organised raffles, barbeques and 'lucky dips' to raise funds to buy learning materials for homework club participants.

'When my daughter moved out of home I found boxes of old books from when she was at kindergarten. It seemed silly to throw them away, so I donated them to the Helpers to use at the homework clubs.' Kara Moon

Current situation and need

In 2013, the Helpers applied for and received an annual grant of $30 000 from the local council (lasting five years), which allowed them to expand their operation and start running homework clubs in several locations throughout Adelaide. At this time, the Helpers also made a decision to incorporate as an incorporated association through Consumer and Business Services (part of the South Australian Government).

Following the formation meeting of the newly-incorporated group, the first committee of management was elected from the original four volunteers with two others who had joined since its establishment:

- Deborah Katz   (a school principal), and
- Warwick McKay (a bookkeeper).

The Helpers' committee met after their formation meeting and elected Kara Moon as the president, Burak Atalay as the secretary and Warwick McKay as the treasurer.

Warwick, who had been looking over the Helpers' financial information, estimated that in the 2013/14 financial year, their taxable income would be $35 000 – meaning that they would have to pay income tax.

He reported this to a committee meeting. Deborah Katz suggested to the committee that the Helpers explore applying for tax exemptions as a charity. She thought that the Helpers would be entitled to register as a charity with the ACNC, which would mean that they would be exempt from paying income tax for the 2014/15 financial year.

'I always thought that to be a charity you had to be working with homeless people or raising money to send to developing countries overseas. I didn't realise that the good work that the Helpers were doing would entitle us to be a charity.' Burak Atalay
Outcome

In February of 2014, the Helpers worked out what they needed to do and applied for registration with the ACNC. About a month later they received a letter confirming that they had been registered as a charity and a charity pack.

Watch the webinar video on what to do before you apply to register with the ACNC

http://www.acnc.gov.au/ACNC/Pblctns/Media_centre/Multimedia/ACNC/Comms/Multimedia/Webinar06072015.aspx

Start your online registration application

Start the online registration application process now (http://acnc.gov.au/ACNC/Register_my_charity/Start_Reg/ACNC/Reg/Apply_to_register.aspx?)

YOUR CHARITY ORGANISATION OBLIGATIONS

In this chapter we discuss what happens once your charity or organisation has been accepted and is now registered.

Information for new charities

Welcome to the ACNC

Congratulations!

Your organisation is now registered as a charity with the ACNC.

Being registered as a charity with the ACNC demonstrates your organisation's commitment to transparency and good governance.

It also means it has some obligations you need to be aware of.

This section will outline your organisation's obligations as a charity, how to fulfil them, and where to get help.

Managing your charity

You can manage all your charity's details online using the ACNC Charity Portal. - https://charity.acnc.gov.au/ACNCPortal/Charity/Sign_In.aspx?

To log in to the Charity Portal you need your charity's username and password. The username is your charity's ABN and the password is in the email they sent your charity upon its successful registration. You can change your charity's password once you log in; you can't change your charity's username though.

Here is a video that is helpful:

https://www.youtube.com/watch?v=BGmlRy57AFA

From within the Charity Portal, you can:

- Check and update your charity's details

- Submit required information

- Print your charity's registration certificate

For more, read our Guide to the ACNC Charity Portal - http://www.acnc.gov.au/
ACNC/Pblctns/Guides/ACNC/Publications/GuidePortal.aspx

Your charity can use the following sentence on public documents (such as
letterheads, emails and websites) to show that it is registered with the ACNC:

- [insert charity name] is registered as a charity with the Australian Charities
  and Not-for-profits Commission ABN [insert 11 digit ABN].

Please note that a registered charity cannot use the ACNC logo.

Guidance for newly registered charities

ACNC Charity Register

Your charity is now listed on the public ACNC Charity Register at acnc.gov.au/
CharityRegister.

Your charity's page on the Charity Register displays important information. This
includes your charity's contact details, its ACNC registration details, copies of its
Annual Information Statements and a list of its 'responsible persons'.

This page acts as your charity's public profile. It is the place where people will go to
find details about your charity, and to verify that it is, in fact, registered.

The Charity Register is used by a wide range of people to check charity details,
including donors, grant-makers, researchers and members of the public, so it is
important to keep your charity's information complete, accurate and up to date.
There is also an obligation for registered charities to keep information up to date by
notifying the ACNC of changes.

When you use the Charity Portal to manage your charity's information, the updates
automatically display on the Charity Register.

For more on the Charity Register, see:

- Information on the ACNC Register - http://www.acnc.gov.au/ACNC/FindCharity/About_Register/ACNC/Reg/Info_Reg.aspx

- Information withheld from the ACNC Register - http://www.acnc.gov.au/ACNC/FindCharity/About_Register/Withheld_info/ACNC/Reg/With_info.aspx

- Understanding financial information on the ACNC Register - http://www.acnc.gov.au/ACNC/FindCharity/About_Register/financial_info/ACNC/Reg/understanding_financial.aspx

- Using the ACNC Register to find information on charities registered with ASIC - http://www.acnc.gov.au/ACNC/Reg/Charityreg.aspx

ACNC obligations

Annual Information Statement:

Each year your charity will be required to submit an Annual Information Statement. Financial information and separate annual financial reports may also be required depending on the size of your charity.

The due date for an Annual Information Statement is six months from the end of your charity's reporting period.

For more information about the Annual Information Statement, visit acnc.gov.au/AIS.

Keeping information up to date:

Your charity has an obligation to notify the ACNC of changes to its details, including its address for service, its responsible people, and its governing documents. Medium and large charities have 28 days to notify the ACNC of any changes and small charities have 60 days.

Notifying the ACNC of changes is done online using the Charity Portal.

For more information about the duty to notify, visit acnc.gov.au/notify.

Keeping records:

Your charity has an obligation to keep records. This includes financial records and operational records.

Records can be kept in any format (including electronically) as long as they are accessible and easy to find. Your charity does not need to provide records to the ACNC unless it is asked to.

For more information about charity record-keeping, visit acnc.gov.au/RecordKeeping.

ACNC Governance Standards:

To remain a registered charity, all charities (except basic religious charities) must comply with the ACNC's Governance Standards. Your charity can choose how it meets each of the governance standards, but it must be able to demonstrate its compliance to the ACNC.

For a list of the five governance standards and details about each one, visit acnc.gov.au/GovernanceStandards.

Useful guides and publications:

- An overview of being registered with the ACNC for charity board or committee members: My charity and the ACNC: a guide for board members - http://www.acnc.gov.au/ACNC/Pblctns/Factsheets/ACNC/FTS/Fact_Board.aspx

- A guide to good governance practices for registered charities: Governance for good: guide for board members - http://www.acnc.gov.au/ACNC/Manage/Tools/ACNC/Edu/Tools/GFG/GFG_Intro.aspx

- A guide to charity fraud and steps your charity can take to protect itself: Protect your charity from fraud: ACNC guide to fraud prevention - http://www.acnc.gov.au/ACNC/Pblctns/Guides/ACNC/Publications/FraudGuide/FraudGuideIntro.aspx

- A guide to managing charity money: Managing charity money – a guide for board members - http://www.acnc.gov.au/ACNC/Publications/Charity_money/Managing_charity_money_-_guide_for_board_members.aspx

- A collection of practical tools and resources, including templates, to help you manage your charity: ACNC tools and resources - http://www.acnc.gov.au/ACNC/Manage/Tools/ACNC/Edu/Tools/MainTools.aspx

Meeting obligations to other regulators

Some charities may continue to have obligations to other federal regulators (such as the ATO or ASIC) or to state and territory regulators. For more information about obligations to other regulators, and for a list of regulators that may affect registered charities, visit acnc.gov.au/OtherRegulators.

Where to get help

The ACNC are available to assist you with managing your charity's registration. You can contact them via:

- phone, weekdays from 9am to 6pm (AEST), on 13 ACNC (13 22 62)
- email at advice@acnc.gov.au
- fax on 1300 232 569, and
- post to ACNC Advice Services, GPO Box 5108, Melbourne, VIC, 3001.

For a full list of their contact details, including social media and other services, visit acnc.gov.au/Contact.

© Commonwealth of Australia 2014

Anh Vo

HOW TO MANAGE YOUR COMMUNITY SUCCESSFULLY

Meeting your obligations is very important. This chapter describes the best way to manage your obligations for your community organisation.

Meet governance standards

Charities must meet ACNC governance standards. These standards set out a minimum standard on how charities should be governed, such as being accountable to members. For full details please see chapter 'Who can Register'.

Keep records - record-keeping for charities registered with the ACNC

Charities must keep records that correctly document and explain their net wealth and performance, and operations, so financial statements can be prepared and to allow for assessment activity.

- What are records?
- How to keep records
- Why keep records?
- Record-keeping for other regulators

Important:

- Charities have different obligations for record-keeping. It depends on your charity's size, its complexity, its activities, how it spends or receives money or other assets and whether it has extra obligations from state-based regulators, such as consumer affairs agencies (for incorporated associations).

- ASIC-registered charities (such as companies limited by guarantee) the ACNC obligations replace requirements that used to apply under the Corporations Act.

- The record- keeping obligations below relate only to requirements under the ACNC Act. Charities may have additional record-keeping requirements under other legislation such as legislation relating to health records, privacy, and so on .

If you are unsure about which financial or operational records your charity should keep, seek professional advice.

Summary of ACNC record-keeping obligations

Your charity:

- must keep certain written financial and operational records

- can keep the records in any format you choose , as long as they are easy to find (including in electronic form)

- can develop its own system or process

- must keep the records for seven years

- must keep records in English, or in a form that can be easily translated to English

- is not required to provide the records to the ACNC unless asked.

What are records?

A record is a piece of information that shows your charity has operated or acted in a particular way, or spent or received money or other assets (made a transaction).

What records to keep for the ACNC

Under the ACNC Act, your charity must keep two types of records:

- financial records, and

- operational records.

Financial records

These must:

- correctly record and explain how your charity spends or receives its money or other assets (transactions)

- correctly record and explain your charity's financial position and performance, and

- allow for true and fair financial statements to be prepared and audited or reviewed, if required.

Even if your charity does not need to submit financial reports to the ACNC (because it is a small or a basic religious charity), your charity still needs to keep financial records that meet these requirements. The ACNC Act or the ACNC Commissioner could require your charity to prepare financial statements.

The ACNC Act does not define what a financial record is. For guidance on what could be a financial record, see examples of financial records below.

A financial record explains your charity's financial activities (transactions), position and performance and examples include:

- **General account books** – including general journal and general and subsidiary ledgers
- **Cash book records** – including receipts and payments
- **Banking records** – including bank and credit card statements, deposit books, cheque butts and bank reconciliations
- **Creditors' records** – including creditors ledger, invoices and paid bills
- **Debtors' records** – including debtors ledger, invoices and receipts
- **Details of any contracts** – including service agreements, office equipment leases, property rental agreements
- **Details of any grant payments and acquittals**
- **Tax invoices and other relevant tax records**
- **Stock records**
- **Records of expenses** – for example, motor vehicle expenses
- **Records of payments relating to employees** – including 'pay as you go' (PAYG) withholding, superannuation and fringe benefits provided
- **Assets list or register**
- **Emails, letters and other communication about finance** – for example, an email about repaying unspent grant funds

Operational records

These are any other documents about your charity's operations. You must keep operational records that show how your charity:

- is entitled to be registered as a charity and as its subtype

- meets its obligations under ACNC Act, and

- meets its obligations under tax law.

The ACNC Act does not define what an operational record is. For guidance on what could be an operational record, see examples of operational records.

An operational record is any information about your charity's activities that shows it complies with the ACNC Act and tax law, and that it continues to be a charity or continues to be entitled to be registered as a particular subtype, for example, as a public benevolent institution (PBI).

Some examples of basic operational records include:

- **Governing documents** – such as a constitution, rules or trust deed

- **Meeting minutes**

- **Operating policies and procedures**

- **Annual reports, donor reports or other reports** – for example on results of programs, projects or services

- **Strategic plans and program plans**

- **Monitoring and evaluation reports**

- **Contracts and agreements** – including funding and other agreements

- **Memoranda of Understanding**

- **Media releases** – such as those released by your charity, and discussing its activities

- **Charity promotional materials** – including pamphlets, posters

- **Any other records to show your charity is working towards its charitable purpose – this includes** electronic, written or multimedia records, for example a short film about your charity's project

How to keep records

Charities can keep the records in any format that suits, as long as they are:

- in writing

- readily accessible (easy to find), and

- in English, or in a form that can be easily translated to English.

Charities can keep records on paper or on their computer (in electronic form).

Tip: To make sure you can provide records if asked, you should back up your computer, and you can also print out a paper record of any important documents. This is because things can go wrong – files can go missing, computers can break or be stolen. When you back your computer up, keep your back-up in a different and secure place to your computer, for example, at a different location.

Keeping paper records

Your charity will have its own systems and processes for keeping paper records. Paper records will include the records you have printed from your computer and other paper records, for example, original receipts and letters you receive in the mail.

Points to remember when keeping paper records

- Organise the paper records into files, boxes, folders or envelopes that allow the records to be found easily

- Separate the different paper records into categories (bank statements, communication, bills, receipts), and

- Separate these records according to your charity's reporting period (for example, financial year 1 July to 30 June).

Why keep records?

When your charity keeps good records of how it is run, this can help you:

- show it is continuing to be run as a not-for-profit and working towards its charitable purposes (and so should remain eligible to be registered as a charity)

- understand whether your charity is in good financial health

- assess whether the right kinds of decisions are being made (operational and financial)

- communicate about your charity's activities and finances

- prepare reports to meet your reporting obligations to the ACNC, other government regulators, donors/funders and members (if relevant), and

- otherwise show that your charity meets its obligations under the ACNC Act, tax and other relevant laws.

Helps to meet the governance standards

Keeping records can also help your charity meet the ACNC governance standards, for example, records can show:

- its charitable purpose and not-for-profit nature (governance standard 1)

- it is being accountable to its members (governance standard 2), and

- it is taking reasonable steps to make sure its responsible persons manage financial affairs responsibly, including not operating the charity whilst it is insolvent (governance standard 5).

Record-keeping for other regulators

Your charity may need to report to other government regulators, which may have their own record-keeping requirements. For example, you will need to maintain good business records to help manage your charity's obligations with the Australian Taxation Office (ATO). If you are following the ACNC record-keeping requirements it is likely that you are meeting most of your obligations to the ATO.

Destruction of records

After seven years (and if your charity has no record-keeping obligations to other regulators), your charity can destroy its records for ACNC purposes. Before you destroy records, check your charity's records policy and other legal obligations, for example, privacy requirements to make sure you are doing so appropriately.

Report Annually

Charities must submit an Annual Information Statement (and, for medium and large sized charities, a financial report) every year, with some exceptions.

Charities have an ongoing obligation to report each reporting period. Charities report by submitting an Annual Information Statement and an annual financial report (if medium or large in size).

Report according to your charity's size

Select your charity size to find out more:

> ### Small charities
> (annual revenue is less than $250 000).

> ### Medium charities
> (annual revenue is $250000 or more, but less than $1 million).

> ### Large charities
> (annual revenue is $1 million or more).

Reporting tasks for charities

- Charity Portal: Request a different reporting period (not 1 July to 30 June)
- Form 4D: Apply to keep charity size [PDF 213KB] (small or medium)
- Charity Portal: Apply to withhold information you submit from the ACNC

Register

- Form 4C: 2014 Annual Information Statement – Bulk lodgement [XLS 744] (more than ten charities), with Form 4C Declaration [PDF 168KB]

- Email ACNC reporting to ask about joint and collective (group) reporting

More information

Related resources – reporting

- Charity size and revenue

- Transitional reporting arrangements

- Withhold information from the ACNC Register

- Reporting due dates

- Cash and accrual accounting

- Review and audit of financial reports

- Financial statements: General and special purpose

- Educational video: Record-keeping and reporting

- Bulk lodgement

- Group reporting

- The National Standard Chart of Accounts (NSCOA)

- 2016 reporting

- 2015 reporting

- 2014 reporting

- 2013 Annual Information Statement guide

- 2013 Annual Information Statement checklist

Related resources – general ACNC

- Charity activities

- [Information on the ACNC Register](#)

- [Information withheld from the ACNC Register](#)

- [ASIC, ORIC and other regulators](#)

- [Basic religious charities](#)

External resources

- OurCommunity: [Damn Good Advice for Treasurers – Twenty-five questions a not-for-profit Treasurer needs to ask](#)

- [CPA Australia:A guide to understanding financial reports of not-for-profit entities](#)

- [CPA Australia: Charities - A guide to financial reporting and assurance requirements](#)

- [Institute of Chartered Accountants Australia (ICAA) - 2016 Reporting guidance](#): Enhancing not-for-profit annual and financial reporting, which includes a supplementary guide for charities reporting under the ACNC Act 2012 (last item in Related Links on the ICAA page)

Keep charity status

Charities must maintain their eligibility to be registered, by remaining not-for-profit, pursuing their charitable purpose and otherwise complying with the ACNC Act.

A charity must make sure it continues to be entitled to registration under the ACNC Act. This includes meeting all of the criteria for initial registration, and ongoing registration, including that it:

- continues to be a charity, which means it must:

  - remain not-for-profit, and

  - have a charitable purpose which is for the public benefit

- is complying with the governance standards (and external conduct standards, if introduced) that may apply to it

- has an Australian Business Number (ABN), and

- is not involved in terrorist or other criminal activity.

Ongoing entitlement as a 'subtype'

A charity must also make sure it continues to meet the description of the 'subtype' of entity (such as a charity for the advancement of education) that it is registered as. This subtype is related to its charitable purpose.

Revocation (cancelling) of charity registration

If a charity loses its entitlement to registration, the ACNC may cancel (revoke) its registration and backdate this to the date it ceased to be eligible. Before taking this action, the ACNC would communicate with the charity and discuss the options available.

If a charity does not meet its obligations, the ACNC focuses on guidance and advice to help it. The ACNC will use their regulatory powers when it is necessary, to maintain public trust and confidence in the sector.

Compliance and enforcement powers

A charity's registration may also be affected if:
- it has breached a section of the ACNC Act (or is more likely than not to), such as failing to notify or report

- it has not complied with a governance or external conduct standard that applies (or is more likely than not to not comply)

- the ACNC discovers that the charity provided information that was false or misleading when it applied for registration

- the registered charity has:

  - a trustee in bankruptcy

  - a liquidator, or

  - a person appointed, or authorised, under an Australian law to manage its affairs because it is unable to pay all its debts as and when they become due and payable.

Read more about the ACNC's approach to regulating charities, and your rights of review and appeal of our decisions at:

https://www.acnc.gov.au/ACNC/About_ACNC/Regulatory_app/ACNC/Regulatory/
Reg_approach.aspx

https://www.acnc.gov.au/ACNC/About_ACNC/Review_Appeals/ACNC/Legal/
Rev_appls.aspx

Duty to notify of failure to meet obligations

You must notify us if you think your charity is not, in a significant way, meeting its ongoing obligations and, as a result, that your charity is no longer entitled to be registered. Under the ACNC Act you must notify us within 28 days of becoming aware of your charity's failure to meet its obligations. For example, if your charity changes its purpose so that it is no longer working towards its charitable purpose.

Read more about your charity's duty to notify - http://www.acnc.gov.au/ACNC/
Manage/UpdateDetails/ACNC/Edu/UpdateNotify.aspx

Voluntary revocation

A charity can choose not to be registered by requesting voluntary revocation and providing reasons. If a charity has its registration revoked, it will no longer receive Commonwealth charity tax concessions or other benefits or exemptions available to registered charities. The ACNC Register will also show that the charity's registration has been revoked.

The ACNC will not automatically approve the request – we must consider a number of factors before cancelling registration.

Ongoing Obligations

Overview of the key legal obligations charities have to the ACNC, including a self-assessment quiz.

All registered charities must meet the following obligations to the ACNC.

Keep charity status

To remain eligible to be registered, charities must continue to be not-for-profit and pursue their charitable purpose or purposes.

Notify ACNC of changes

Charities must notify the ACNC if any of the following details change:

- legal name

- address for service (where legal documents can be sent)

- 'responsible persons' (people who are members of your charity's governing body including directors or committee members, or its trustees) – you need to let them know if someone takes on or finishes the role of a responsible person, and

- governing documents (such as its constitution, rules or trust deed).

You must also let them know if you think your charity is not meeting its ongoing obligations to the ACNC in a significant way, and as a result, your organisation is no longer entitled to be registered.

Keep records

Charities must keep financial records that correctly record and explain their transactions and financial position (net wealth) and performance and enable true and fair financial statements to be prepared and to be audited, if required. They must also keep operational records which explain their activities.

Report information annually

Charities (except corporations registered with the Office of the Registrar of Indigenous Corporations) must submit an Annual Information Statement (and, for medium and large charities, a financial report) every year. This statement is due within six months of the end of your reporting period and can be submitted by using the ACNC Charity Portal.

Meet the governance standards

Charities (except a limited group called 'basic religious charities') must comply with the governance standards. These standards set out a minimum standard of governance, to help promote public trust and confidence in charities.

Unless we tell you otherwise, these ACNC obligations are **in addition to** any other obligations your charity has under other laws or to other Commonwealth, state and territory regulators. For example, if your charity is an incorporated association you will still have to report to your state or territory regulator for incorporated associations. The ACNC is working with other government departments and agencies to reduce regulatory burden for charities. Read more about the ACNC's work in red tape reduction on the website.

Update charity details

Charities have a duty to notify the ACNC of changes, including to charity details, responsible people and governing documents and of any breach of the ACNC Act, including governance standards.

Duty to notify of changes

Charities have a duty to notify the ACNC of changes to their details, including responsible people and governing documents. Once you are aware of the change, you must notify the ACNC of changes as soon as you reasonably can but no later than:

- 28 days (medium and large charities), or
- 60 days (small charities).

Administrative penalties may apply for failing to notify the ACNC.

Use the ACNC Charity Portal

Keep details up-to-date and lodge forms through the Charity Portal https://charity.acnc.gov.au/ACNCPortal/Charity/Sign_In.aspx?WebsiteKey=15ae55d1-4f4a-4d80-9549-6ea9d089c234&returnurl=%2f

Update your charity subtype

Some charities registered before 31 December 2013 must update their charity subtypes (reflecting their charitable purpose) by 30 June 2015.
See 'Tools to help manage your charity'.

Tools and resources

Guides, quick tips and other tools and resources to help you run your charity.
http://www.acnc.gov.au/ACNC/Edu/Tools/MainTools.aspx

Factsheet - Schools, universities and education providers

This factsheet provides information for schools, universities and other education providers who may wish to register as charities with the ACNC.

The ACNC registers organisations as charities. Schools and universities that meet the legal meaning of charity and their requirements for registration can register as charities with the ACNC.

Can government schools and education providers register with the ACNC?

Organisations that are run by the government are generally not considered to be charitable. Because they are not charities, government schools and institutions generally cannot register with the ACNC. In particular, government schools would likely fall within the definition of 'government entity' in the *Charities Act 2013* (Cth), and therefore, be excluded from the definition of 'charity'.

Can non-government schools, universities and other education providers register with the ACNC?

Other education providers may meet the ACNC's registration requirements. Examples of education providers that can register include:

- non-government schools
- universities

- schools operated by religious organisations

- schools for specific training (such as language schools), and

- kindergartens and other pre-schools.

When applying to register, education providers may wish to select purpose of 'advancing education' as their charitable purpose and 'educational activities' as one of their charitable activities. Education providers may also select other recognised charitable purposes they have, or other charitable activities they engage in, such as community welfare activities or scholarly research.

What obligations do registered charities have to the ACNC?

Education providers registered with the ACNC have ongoing obligations under the ACNC Act. These include to:

- notify us of certain changes

- keep records

- report to us each year

- comply with governance standards and external conduct standards, where applicable.

What if my school, university or other education provider already has to report to another government agency?

The ACNC is working to reduce this regulatory burden for charities. We have entered into a number of agreements with agencies that provide for cooperation and exchange of information, such as with the Tertiary Education Quality and Standards Agency (TEQSA).

Your school may be required by Australian law to prepare financial reports on a calendar year basis (1 January to 31 December) instead of the ACNC Act's usual reporting period of 1 July to 30 June. They call this a 'different reporting period' or a substituted accounting period.

The ACNC will approve this calendar year as a different reporting period if your school notifies the ACNC that the law requires reporting on this basis. You can apply for a different reporting period through the Charity Portal, and including this legal requirement as the reason for your request.

What if my non-government school reports to the Department of Education and Training?

For the 2014 and 2015 reporting periods, non-government schools do not have to provide financial information to them directly. Read more about the non-government schools transitional reporting arrangements.

What will happen to my school building fund – will it be registered with the ACNC?

If your school building fund was recognised (endorsed) as a charity by the Australian Taxation Office (ATO) to receive charity tax concessions (such as goods and services tax concessions) before 3 December 2012, it will have automatically have been registered with the ACNC. Check the ACNC Register to see if your school building fund is registered.

If your school building fund is not registered and has deductible gift recipient (DGR) status, it may need to register with the ACNC so it can continue to receive tax deductible donations. Your fund needs to register with the ACNC if it is an 'ACNC type of entity'.

Please Note: The deadline to register with them (if needed) has now expired. If your school building fund has DGR status and is not a registered charity, contact the ATO to confirm whether you need to register.

School building funds for government schools do not need to be registered with the ACNC to apply to the ATO for DGR.

Read the ATO guidance on:

• DGRs (see the DGR table which lists which DGR categories need to register)

- working out whether your fund is an 'ACNC type of entity':

  - ATO Interpretative Decision 2013/60

  - ATO Interpretative Decision 2013/61

  - ATO Interpretative Decision 2013/62

What if I want to set up a school building fund?

School building funds that meet the legal meaning of charity and the
ACNC requirements for registration can register as charities with the ACNC.
Charities must be registered with the ACNC to access charity tax concessions. If
your school building fund wants to apply for DGR status, it will need to be registered
with the ACNC if it is an 'ACNC type of entity'. Read the ATO's guidance above for
more information.

Manage my charity type - http://www.acnc.gov.au/ACNC/Edu/ManageType.aspx

Some charity types have similar obligations, due to their legal structure (such as
incorporated associations) or what they do. Find your type.

Factsheet - Overseas aid and development charities - http://www.acnc.gov.au/ACNC/FTS/Overseas_charities.aspx

This factsheet contains information for overseas aid and development organisations
who wish to register or are already registered with the ACNC.

List of regulators that may affect charities - http://www.acnc.gov.au/ACNC/Site/Regulator_list.aspx

List of regulators that charities may have obligations to, including ASIC, ORIC and
state and territory regulators.

ASIC, ORIC and other regulators - http://www.acnc.gov.au/ACNC/Edu/ASIC_othrRegs.aspx

Information about the obligations charities have to other regulators, such as ASIC, ORIC, the ATO and state and territory incorporated association and fundraising regulators.

Aboriginal and Torres Strait Islander corporations - http:// www.acnc.gov.au/ACNC/Edu/ATSIcorps.aspx

Information for organisations registered under the CATSI Act as a corporation, as well as with the ACNC as a charity.

Factsheet - Registrable Australian bodies and the ACNC - http:// www.acnc.gov.au/ACNC/FTS/Fact_RAB.aspx

This factsheet explains changes for registrable Australian bodies that are registered with the ACNC

Companies limited by guarantee - http://www.acnc.gov.au/ACNC/ Edu/CLG.aspx

Information about starting a charitable company limited by guarantee and its obligations to ASIC and the ACNC.

Wind up, merge or change legal structure

Information about what to do if you decide to wind up (close) your charity, merge with another charity or change its legal structure.

You may change your charity by:

- winding up (closing) your charity

- merging your charity with another charity, or

- continuing your charity with a different legal structure.

Wind up your charity

You may choose to wind up your charity for many reasons. This is called voluntarily winding up. You may also be forced to wind up your charity if it is insolvent (unable to pay all of its debts when they are due) or does not comply with certain important legal requirements. This is called compulsory winding up.

When winding up your charity, the main things you need to know are that:

- you may need to get professional advice about winding up your charity

- you must follow your governing documents and all legal obligations (including those of your incorporating regulator) that are relevant to winding up your charity

- you must tell people that your charity is winding up, including people you have contracts with, members, donors, any employees

- your charity must remain solvent (able to pay all of its debts when they are due) while you are winding up

- you must cancel your registration with the ACNC if you wind up your charity, and

- if you have wound up your registered charity, it will remain on the ACNC Register but will be identified as no longer registered.

Merge your charity

You may wish to merge your charity with another registered charity that has similar purposes, beneficiaries (people it helps) and activities. You may choose to do this for a number of reasons, such as to share resources or to broaden your charity's reach.

When merging your charity, the main things you need to know are that:

- you may need to get professional advice about merging your charity

- you must follow your governing documents and all legal obligations (including those of your incorporating regulator) that are relevant to merging your charity

- you must tell people if your charity is merging, including people you have contracts with, members, donors, any employees

- merging may affect your charity registration and any tax concessions you have, and

- you may have legal obligations to your incorporating regulator, the Australian Business Register (ABR), the Australian Taxation Office (ATO) and the ACNC.

Change your charity's legal structure

You may wish to continue your charity but change its legal structure (for example, incorporate your unincorporated charity, so that you can open a bank account, provide better legal liability protection for your members and enter into agreements in the charity's name instead of an individual's name).

If you change your charity's legal structure, you may need to:

- advise us of the change of legal structure using Form 3B: Change of charity details

- change your charity's details on the Charity Portal (for changes to responsible persons and address details and to upload new or amended governing documents only)

- apply to register a new charity, and/or

- apply to revoke the registration of (deregister) an existing charity.

You may also need to do other things, such as notify the relevant incorporating regulator(s) or register or cancel an Australian Business Number (ABN) with the Australian Business Register.

See their guidance on changing your charity's legal structure below:

Change to ABN

If your charity has a new ABN, and no other changes have occurred, please complete Form 3B: Change of charity details to notify the ACNC. If other changes have occurred, such as the charity has a new legal structure, changed its charitable purposes, or merged with another entity, then you will need to provide the ACNC with additional information.

Anh Vo

*See the table below for more information.

Legal structure

Charities may change their legal structure for a variety of reasons. It may be because you wish to:

- incorporate your unincorporated charity (for example, so that you can open a bank account, provide better legal liability protection for your members and enter into agreements in the charity's name instead of an individual's name)

- incorporate as a company with the Australian Securities and Investment Commission (for example, because your charity has become larger and wants to operate across Australia and overseas)

- merge your charity with another charity (for example, because you have a similar purpose and want to share resources), or

- register your charity with the Office of the Registrar of Indigenous Corporations, so that you can apply for certain government grants for indigenous charities. For more information, see the federal government's Indigenous Advancement Strategy (as at July 2014).

In many cases this will not mean you are required to re-register with the ACNC.

Please see the table below for guidance:

Type of Change	Action Required
Unincorporated entity to an incorporated or company structure without changes to purposes	Complete *Form 3B: Change of charity details* and include copy of new governing document.
Incorporated entity to company structure or Registrable Australian Body without changes to purposes	Complete *Form 3B: Change of charity details* and include copy of new governing document.

Incorporated or company structure to unincorporated entity without changes to purposes	Complete *Form 3B: Change of charity details* and include copy of new governing document.We may also ask for additional information.
Charities merging and creating a new legal entity	New registration application required for new entity, and complete *Form 5A: Application to revoke charity registration* to revoke the original charity.

© Commonwealth of Australia 2014

The following is an excerpt from the following site https://www.consumer.vic.gov.au/clubs-and-not-for-profits/fundraisers that describes how fundraisers should be registered and the proper use of monies associated with them:

A beneficiary is a person or group who will receive money or other benefits from your fundraising activities.

It is important that you identify your beneficiary clearly on your registration application. This information will appear on the public register and will give the public confidence in donating to your appeal.

When applying for registration, you must provide one of the following:

*•	The name of every person or organisation that will benefit from the fundraising appeal. You must also provide a letter of consent from each beneficiary.*

*•	A description of a group of beneficiaries who share common characteristics. This is acceptable when individual names are not available. You must attach an additional page with a detailed description of the group. (For example, identifying 'orphaned and disadvantaged children' as a group of beneficiaries is not sufficient. You would need to identify a specific orphanage that cares for children, or specific programs for disadvantaged children in a particular locality or region.)*

*•	A description of the cause for which the appeal is to be conducted. This is acceptable when the appeal is not being conducted for the immediate direct benefit of one or more people; for example, an appeal for funds for medical research.*

You can name yourself as a beneficiary (though not as the sole beneficiary). However, we will examine your application to determine if the fundraising is in the public interest.

Anh Vo

Commercial fundraisers that raise funds on behalf of other fundraisers should name as a beneficiary each principal fundraiser they have an agreement with, and state the percentage of funds each will receive.

CONCLUSION

The aim of this book is to help people understand how to setup and run a Not for Profit organisation successfully with the all the right intentions to help their local community.

It is important to make sure that the right people are in charge of projects where there is money involved. The use of other peoples money whether it is grants from the government or from members of the public, it should be used with full honesty and integrity. It should be used for the utmost benefit of the recipients for which it was first intended.

If you know of any under handed activities in your local community, you should stand up and say something! Together we can stop the people that are doing the wrong thing by the right people!

Always remember…

Unfortunately there are people that abuse the system which makes it hard for those that want to do the right thing by themselves, their family, and their country…For these people we want you to please remember the following:

'If you aren't happy here then LEAVE. We didn't force you to come here. You asked to be here. So accept the country YOU accepted.'

Again, we ask that you don't bring an old war to a new country, keep Australia peaceful.

Important notes to remember and understand for those people that come from other countries:

It is not an advantage to use charities for the purpose of political activities or complaints. Please see below the list of points that outline this:

- The Local City Council recognised the flag, the flag of your old country across the Pacific Ocean and the Australian National Flag

- Complaints with the Congressman, Federal State Parliament of Australia to interfere with democracy, human rights and also overthrow the Government of another country (where you came from)

- You taking advantage of the freedom protest of Australia, holding the flag and group of people beyond the protesters that vandalised the honest business of Australian citizens (Restaurant, reception Manager, live shows, singer)

- Blackmail: killing, violence, burned a business to cause fear for the public

- Abusing fraudulent charity funding and government grants

- Taking advantage of charity; disaster, fire ,flood storm ... fundraising appeal to the public and misuse of funds

- The head of the charity should remember that Government grants are from tax contributions from Australian citizens

- Scamming of grants means that you are stealing from all Australian citizens

You were asked by the Government to accept the rules and conditions when you came here to settle, and become an Australian citizen, which means you must contribute to the public society of Australia.

You always complained about what happened in your old country ... saying it is the best way ... you should leave here and go back to where you came from if you are not happy with how it is run here. The Australian Government do not have the duty of responsibility to take care of other countries, it is for those people to solve it.

Please remember, the Prime Minister, Premiers, Ministers Members of the Lower House, Senators of State ad Federal of Australia are NOT INTERNATIONAL POLICE.

Perhaps the message is that the State and Federal Governments in Australia should cease funding to certain associations as it uses taxpayer's money which provides full-time political activities. In all instances, they must work as a charity and be registered with the ACNC.

One of my experiences in particular was with a chapter where all they complained about was the state of the Federal government of Australia and the trouble they had compared to what happened in their own country. It is important to realise that it is not the governments fault. It is your responsibility to understand what happens in this country (Australia) and deal with the rules and regulations in accordance with the constitution of this country.

RESOURCES

- ATO: Guidance for non-profits

- Fundraising Institute of Australia (peak body) – see its Principles & Standards of Fundraising Practice

- Community Door (managed by QCOSS with Queensland government funding – with multi-lingual resources about starting an organisation)

- National Pro Bono Resource Centre

- Not-for-profit Law @ Justice Connect (NSW and Victorian site with general information for not-for-profits, including information on getting started)

- Not for Profit Compliance Support Centre (Victorian site with general information)

Registering with the ACNC

Information about the requirements for registration, and who can register with the ACNC.

- Charity subtypes and charitable purpose
- Factsheet - Governing documents
- Before you start a charity - checklist
- Registration checklist
- Factsheet - Responsible persons - board or committee members
- Factsheet - Indigenous corporations – applying for charity registration with the ACNC
- Factsheet - Address For Service
- Factsheet - Who can register with the ACNC

State and territory and other regulators of charities

Information about the obligations your charity may have to (and benefits from) other Commonwealth, state or local government agencies.

List of regulators in Australia that may affect charities

ASIC, ORIC and other regulators

Charity tax concessions and other benefits

Information about the various Commonwealth tax concessions and benefits available to registered charities, as well as benefits (such as deductible gift recipient status) that may depend on registration.

- Factsheet - Charity tax concessions available
- Factsheet - Deductible gift recipients (DGRs) and the ACNC
- Factsheet - Other Commonwealth concessions, benefits and exemptions

Information by charity type

Information for particular types of charities, according to their legal structure (trusts), their purpose or sector.

- Factsheet - Trusts and the ACNC
- Companies limited by guarantee
- Factsheet - Unincorporated associations and ACNC registration
- Factsheet - Schools, universities and education providers
- Factsheet - Arts associations
- Factsheet - Private and public ancillary funds
- Factsheet - Environmental groups
- Factsheet - Childcare organisations
- Factsheet - Public benevolent institution?
- Factsheet - Animal welfare groups
- Factsheet - Self help groups
- Factsheet - Overseas aid and development charities
- Factsheet - Hospitals and healthcare providers
- Factsheet - Social clubs
- Factsheet - Housing providers
- Factsheet - Registrable Australian bodies and the ACNC
- Factsheet - Sporting groups
- Factsheet - Health promotion charities
- Factsheet - Religious charities

Successfully Changing Lives by Building a Community

Managing your charity's duties

Information about the duties of charities to the ACNC, including meeting governance standards and other reporting annually.

- Factsheet - Mapping the ACNC governance standards to the CMA Standards Council Principles and Standa
- Fundraising: people in vulnerable circumstances
- Charity pack - Welcome to the ACNC
- Managing charity money - guide for board members
- Webinar - Welcome to the board 9 November 2015
- Factsheet - Comply with the CMA Standards Council Principles and Standards
- Governance standard myths
- Record keeping checklist
- My charity and the ACNC - guide for board members
- Ongoing obligations
- Factsheet - Mapping ACNC governance standards to the ACFID Code of Conduct

Good governance tips and guides

Tips and information for charities on key charity management topics and situations.

- Changing your governing rules - incorporated
- Overseas aid charities and terrorist financing
- Choosing a new board member
- Internal disputes
- Managing people's information and data
- Holding meetings
- Disaster relief
- Changing your governing rules - unincorporated
- Protect your charity from fraud guide - the ACNC guide to fraud prevention
- Managing conflicts of interest - guide for charity board members
- Having strong financial controls
- Governance for good - a guide for board members
- Engaging volunteers
- Working with fundraising agencies
- Holding your annual general meeting
- Taking on employees

- <u>Conflicts of interest</u>
- <u>Charity reserves: financial stability and sustainability</u>

Understanding charity impact

Information for the public about steps they can take to understand information about charities and make informed decisions when donating or volunteering.

<u>FAQs: Charities and fundraising</u>
These FAQs are for people who want information about how charities can raise and spend funds.

<u>FAQs: Charities and administration costs</u>
These FAQs provide an overview of the realities of charity administration costs.

<u>Information on the Register - understanding financial information</u>
When deciding whether to donate to or volunteer for a charity, the financial information on the ACNC Register provides a basis for understanding the charity and its activities in greater detail.

<u>Charity money myths - the facts about operating as a not-for-profit</u>
This factsheet corrects a number of myths about operating as a not-for-profit, including that charities can't make a profit, invest or incur administration costs.

<u>Understanding charity impact</u>
If you are donating to a charity, you may wish to make sure that your donation is creating the greatest impact possible.

<u>Making sure your donation gets to where it needs to</u>
Joint ACNC and QUT factsheet giving steps to help make sure your donation is going where it is intended.

<u>Are there too many charities in Australia?</u>
An information sheet and set of FAQs that explores the number of charities in Australia.

Video - Protect yourself from charity scams
ACNC video on how to protect yourself from charity scams.

Charities and administration costs
A factsheet jointly produced by the ACNC and the Queensland University of Technology about administration costs for charities.

The following link is a great for publications and resources that can help with a variety of questions you may have:

http://www.acnc.gov.au/ACNC/Pblctns/Pubs_resources/ACNC/Publications/Publctn.aspx?Noleft=1&hkey=ba87971c-dd4a-4af7-a649-74c8f936eaa1

© Commonwealth of Australia 2014

ABOUT THE AUTHOR

Anh was born and grew up at the beginning of the "First Vietnam war" which started in 1946, he was just seven years old. This war was started by Mr. Ho Chi Minh who was a member of Third International Communist Party Leader of Vietnamese Communist who went into battle with the French in 1953.

After Anh returned from National service in the Vietnam war he worked for the Military Assistant Command Vietnam (MACV). After 27th March 1973 the MACV no longer operated in Vietnam and he was transferred to work for the Defense Attache Office Saigon (DAO Saigon).

In the refugee camp in Indonesia he worked as an unpaid volunteer for the United Nation High Commission of Refugee at Galang Camp that included the American delegation of Joint Volunteer Agency (JVA) and the Australian delegation in helping file forms and as a basic interpreter.

Life in Vietnam was very hard and he just knew there had to be something better than this for his family and himself. His goal in life was to be able to provide a good and happy life for his family in a new country.

On 23rd September 1984 they arrived at the Midway Hostel Immigration in Maribyrnong in Victoria where he worked as an unpaid volunteer with the Sister Power Catholic Immigration in Melbourne to help the new people that arrived in Australia.

Since coming to Australia, he has achieved many wonderful achievements that would not have been possible in his country; Anh says 'THANK YOU AUSTRALIA for giving me the opportunity'.

Below are achievements and contributions he has made to this wonderful country of ours that he now calls home - Australia:

-Setup a Vietnamese Volunteer Group in 1997 (Hoi Thien Chí Ty Nan Viet Nam) to call the Australian citizens of Vietnamese background to contribute their time to become involved as follows in community activities organised for :

-Clean Up Australia Day

-Royal Children Hospital Good Friday Appeal

-The Management of The Herald Sun newspaper gave our group the use of their head office to fundraise by Radio (permission granted by Mr Quang Luu Director of SBS radio for the Vietnamese language in Australia) he allowed us to seek donations for the Royal Melbourne Children Good Friday Appeal via the SBS Broadcast program "Adaft" from Channel 7 and 101FM that continued for 4 years (1998 through to 2001) at the Sun Herald Office.

-Plant 300 trees at Sunshine Hospital

-Former member of Cleaning and Greening of Maribyrnong City Council

-Involved in the Volunteer Group for Clean Up Australia Day from 1997

Others communities:

- Member of Lions Club of Footscray 1989 (13 years)

- Former Board of Director Lions Club of Footscray

- IM foundered Lions Club of Melbourne Vietnamese

-Former Member - Board of Director Westgate Community Inc.

(Organisation activities : To train people of long term unemployment; part time volunteer work (unpaid), my position was The Sounding Board and Mentoring NEIS Program member Steering Committee)

-Member of the Vietnamese Community In Australia Victoria Chapter Inc.

-Founder of Vietnamese Volunteer Group (Hội Thiên Chí Ty Nạn)

Anh Vo

AWARDS Received:

-1998 Maribyrnong City Council Civic Awards Environmental

-2001 Royal Childrens Hospital Good Friday Appeal DISTINGUISHED SERVICES AWARD

-Victorian Multicultural Commission International Year of Volunteers 2001 "In Recognition of Your Nomination "

-Premier Award to the group "Hoi Thien Chi Ty Nan In recognition of voluntary International Tear of Volunteers 2001" Signed by The Hon. Steve Bracks MP Premier Of Victoria and The Hon. Christine Campbell MP, Minister For Community Services

-The Vietnamese Community In Victoria Chapter Inc Award for Mr An Long Vo (Anh Vo) for Excellences Leadership Services signed By Mr Phong Nguyen President of the VCA/and The Hon Christine Campbell Minister for Community Services

Anh Vo

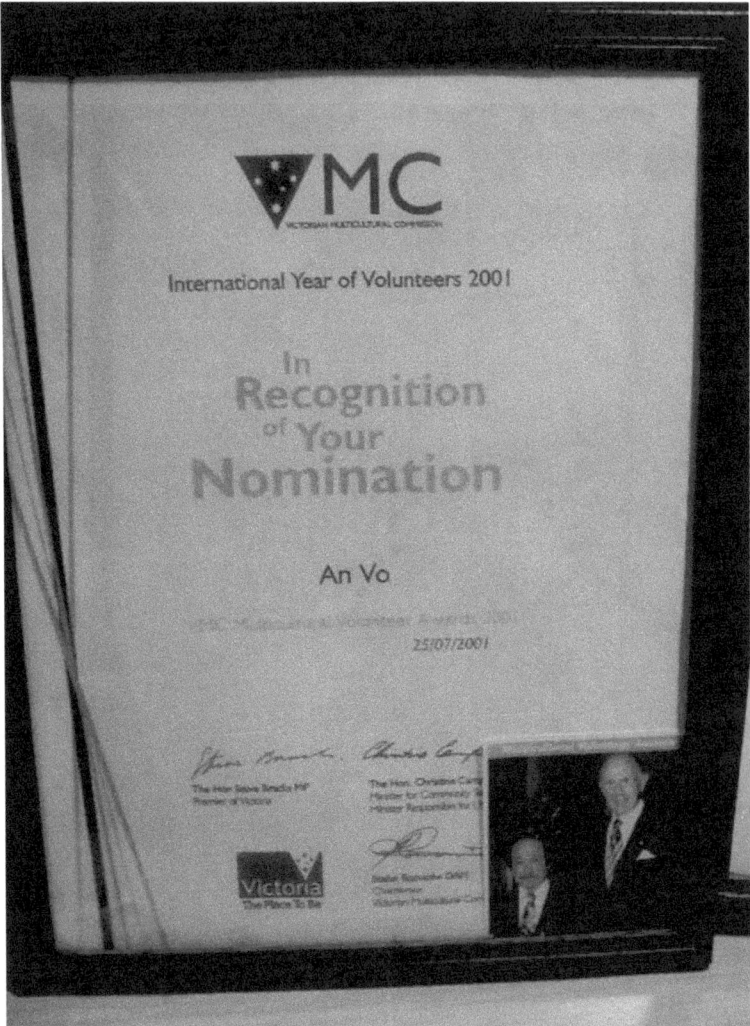

Photo Anh Vo vs Sir John Landy Governor of Victoria Premier Awards to group

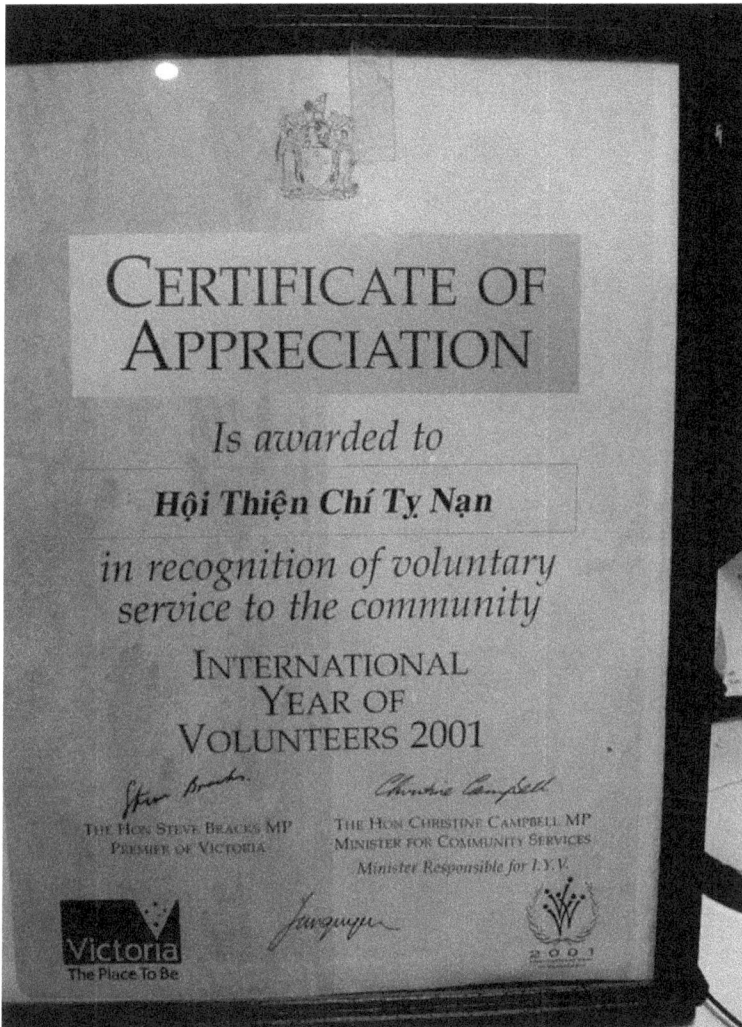

CERTIFICATE OF
APPRECIATION

Is *awarded to*

Hội Thiện Chí Tỵ Nạn

*in recognition of voluntary
service to the community*

INTERNATIONAL
YEAR OF
VOLUNTEERS 2001

THE HON STEVE BRACKS MP
PREMIER OF VICTORIA

THE HON CHRISTINE CAMPBELL MP
MINISTER FOR COMMUNITY SERVICES
Minister Responsible for I.Y.V.

Victoria
The Place To Be

2001

Anh Vo

Multicultural **Victoria**

Volume 5 No 2 - Spring 2001 - ISSN 1321 9340 - A publication of the Victorian Multicultural Commission

A very busy time for the VMC

As the term of this Commission comes to a close, much of the work and planning of the past four years comes to fruition and the goals this VMC set for itself are realised. The front cover of this edition of *Multicultural Victoria* illustrates some of this work and many of the activities the Commission undertook in July and August 2001.

Change of Culture – Government Responding to All Victorians

This paper, prepared by the Commission and presented to Government, is an outcome of the close, cooperative working relationship the VMC has had with government and government departments during its term.

This paper was written to stimulate discussion - and should be read in this spirit.

Reporting back sessions

At the beginning of its 2000-2001 consultation program, the Commission made a commitment to communities that, at the end of the process, it would report back on the outcomes of the issues raised and the responses of government to these issues. Such sessions have now taken place in Shepparton, Bendigo, Albury Wodonga, Mildura, LaTrobe Valley, Ballarat, Geelong and in metropolitan Melbourne.

VMC Community Grants Program

The Commission's 2000-2001 grants program was reshaped to include categories of funding that better reflect the needs of communities. Below is one of the cheque presentation ceremonies conducted by Members of Parliament and the Commission for this program. See page 16 for more pictures.

Multicultural Volunteer Awards

The awards presentation ceremony was hosted by the Governor of Victoria on 25 July at Government House. For more information on the Multicultural Volunteer Awards, see the article on page 3 of this edition.

Round Table on Diversity

Round Table on Diversity, hosted by the Governor of Victoria at Government House on 8 August. More information about this event is contained in an article on pages 4-6 of this edition.

Anh Vo with Sir John Landy, Governor of Victoria Multicultural Awards 2001 Year of International Volunteer at Government House

Anh Vo from right, Mr Quang Lưu Director of BSB Radio first second row from left and volunteer team Herald Sun Head Office on Good Friday Appeal for Royal Children Hospital 1999 and Anh's son Phuong Vo fro, left second row and Mr Hung Chau Vice President of VCA Vic

Anh Vo

VMC Multicultural Volunteer Awards

The VMC Multicultural Volunteer Awards (see autumn 2001 edition of *Multicultural Victoria*) were presented at a delightful function held at Government House on 25 July 2001. His Excellency, John Landy, AC, MBE, Governor of Victoria, hosted the function and, together with the Hon Steve Bracks, Premier of Victoria, presented the Awards.

All those nominated for the awards received Volunteer Certificates and the following organisations and individuals were presented with awards:

Organisations - Cultural Awareness Initiatives Award
North Yarra Community Health Multicultural Communities Association, Eritrean Community in Australia Inc, Jewish Museum of Australia, NESB LINKS Inc, Victorian Arabic Social Services, Ethnic Council of Shepparton & District, Australia Burma Society

Organisations - Inclusive Practices or Initiatives Award
Ballarat Regional Multicultural Council

Individuals - Volunteer Involvement Award
Dalia Antanaitis, Jean Bowen, Agata Formica, Virginia Hocking, Al-Amin Idris, Engeliena Jager, Evangeline Lennie, Lilliana Marchesi, Morley Pereira, Julie Roberts, Masha Zeleznikow

Individuals - Youth Award
Vytas Brazaitis, Melissa De Matteo, Liliana Sanelli, Kim Nguyen

Premier's Special Commendation Award
Melbourne Lithuanian Choir 'Dainos Samburis', Chev Joseph Saviour Attard AM, JP, KCSt J, Silvana D'Ambrosio, Edith Dizon-Fitzsimmons, Rolando Garay, Salvatrice Marotta, Carmen Testa OAM

The VMC and Volunteering Victoria were delighted with the response to the awards program, especially as the more than 200 nominations came from rural and regional Victoria as well as metropolitan Melbourne, and were fairly evenly divided between men and women and across age groups. It was also pleasing to see the range of large and smaller communities involved in the individual and organisational nominations.

■ His Excellency, John Landy, AC, MBE, Governor of Victoria with one of the recipients of the Multicultural Volunteer Awards

Farewell and welcome

Commissioners Hass Dellal OAM, Max Petterlin and Chin Tan will leave the VMC on the 31 August 2001 at the end of the term of the current VMC. The contribution these men have made to the work of the Commission has been extraordinary.

Despite their professional full-time responsibilities – Hass is Executive Director of the Australian Multicultural Foundation, Max is a company director in the food service industry and previously practiced law; and Chin is a barrister and solicitor of the Supreme court – they have been unstinting in the time and energy they have devoted to the activities of the VMC. All involved in the area of multicultural affairs thank you!

On 2 August, the Premier, Steve Bracks, announced that Mr George Lekakis would succeed Mr Stefan Romaniw OAM as Chairperson of the Victorian Multicultural Commission. The current Commission would like to congratulate Mr Lekakis on this appointment.

Mr Lekakis has been Chairperson of the Ethnic Communities' Council of Victoria since 1997 and will take up his new post on September 1.

Mr Bracks said Mr Lekakis brought a wealth of knowledge and experience that would further enhance Victoria's reputation as Australia's most tolerant and multicultural State.

'The Victorian Multicultural Commission plays an important role in providing Government with independent advice on issues affecting Victorians from culturally and linguistically diverse backgrounds,' Mr Bracks said.

The exiting Chairperson and Commissioners have made an undertaking to continue to work closely with the new Commission.

Anh's son Phuong Vo recipient of Victorian Multicultural Award 2001 year of International Volunteer with His Excellency Sir John Landy, Governor of Victoria

VMC

VICTORIAN MULTICULTURAL COMMISSION

International Year of Volunteers 2001

In Recognition of Your Nomination

Phuong Vo

VMC Multicultural Volunteer Awards 2001

25/07/2001

The Hon Steve Bracks MP
Premier of Victoria

The Hon. Christine Campbell MP
Minister for Community Services
Minister Responsible for I.Y.V.

Victoria
The Place To Be

Stefan Romaniw OAM
Chairperson
Victorian Multicultural Commission

Anh Vo

amnesty international australia

ACN 002 806 233

14 Risley Street   PO Box 1333   T : 03 9427 7055
Richmond   Richmond North 3121   F : 03 9427 1643
                                          E : vicaia@ozemail.com.au

25 November 1999

Mr Anh Vo
4 Gibbs Street
Maidstone VIC 3012

Dear Anh,

Thanks so much for your call yesterday. I enclose a number of Amnesty International membership forms. Unfortunately we do not have those in Vietnamese: something we are working on!

I also enclose copies of our flier for the Human Rights Day Event on 5/12//99. I was delighted to hear that you and your Human Rights group would be participating. I thank you for your suggestion regarding how this event could be publicised within the Vietnamese community. I would be grateful if you could go ahead and arrange for mention of the event in Vietnamese newspaper and on community radio.

Thanks so much and I look forward to working with you and your group.

Yours sincerely,

Carolyn Graydon
Regional Coordinator

small change can make a big difference ⚡ candle day – october 22nd &23rd

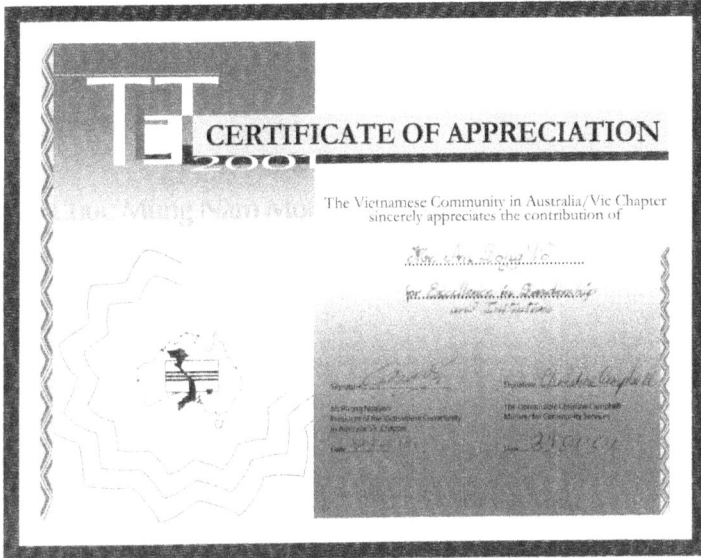

CERTIFICATE OF APPRECIATION

The Vietnamese Community in Australia/Vic Chapter
sincerely appreciates the contribution of

Anh Vo

Good
Friday
Appeal
ROYAL CHILDREN'S HOSPITAL

March 24, 1999

Founded by
The Herald and Weekly Times
in 1931

Level 2 IBM Centre
60 City Road Southbank
Victoria 3006 Australia

PO Box 14744
Melbourne City MC
Victoria 8001

Telephone 03) 9292 1166
Facsimile   03) 9292 2650

Anh Vo
4 Gibb Street
MAIDSTONE. VIC 3012

Dear Anh,

Thank you so much for your hospitality on Friday night. It was wonderful to have the opportunity to meet with your committee, distinguished members of your community.

We are the Good Friday Appeal are very excited at the opportunity to have you all as a part of our Appeal family.

I'm sure together we will do great things for the Royal Children's Hospital.

With best wishes.

Christine Unsworth Screen,
EXECUTIVE DIRECTOR.

Enc. Copy of letter received from Tuong Quang Lug

lifestart

f o u n d a t i o n

Wishes to thank you

Anh Vo

for your valuable contribution

and ongoing support.

Karen Leonard
Lifestart Foundation

2005

Anh Vo

UnitingCare

Outreach Mission
Footscray-Yarraville Outreach ABN 16 764 349 334
The Uniting Church in Australia
Offering free and confidential help to all in need

Celebrating 30 Years

93 Geelong Road
FOOTSCRAY VIC 3011

P.O. Box 4132
WEST FOOTSCRAY VIC 3012
TELEPHONE: 9689 3515
9687 1077
FACSIMILE: 9396 1018
EMAIL:
ucafoots@alphalink.com.au

6th January, 2004

Anh Vo,
4 Gibb Street,
Maidstone, 3012

Dear Friend,

Please accept our thanks and appreciation for the generous contribution you made toward our Christmas Family Fun Day. Making the drinks available made a significant contribution the children's enjoyment.

Being a charitable organization it is sometimes difficult to find the funds to stage events like our Christmas Family Fun Day. It is good that there are people such as you who make such generous gifts. The families who have used our emergency relief services during the year really appreciate the chance to get out and have some Christmas fun.

Thank you once again for your contribution, and for thinking about us and those who are less fortunate.

Yours sincerely

Richard Arnold
Director

A Community Service of the Footscray-Yarraville Parish

Successfully Changing Lives by Building a Community

Compuskill
Information
Technology
Centre

22 Hopkins Street
Footscray Victoria 3011
Facsimile (03) 689 9093
Telephone (03) 279 0100

Friday June 14th 1996

Anh Vo
4 Gibbs Street
MAIDSTONE 3012

Dear Anh

I would like to thank you for your involvement on the Vietnamese Steering Committee. Without your help and commitment we would not have been able to get the course established and running so well.

I am pleased to inform you that eight businesses were approved by the DEETYA Advisory Panel to begin NEIS income support immediately and a further nine were approved with conditions attached. We are very pleased with this result and are confident that the participants will establish successful businesses.

I look forward to continuing our relationship in the future and thank you again for all your time and effort.

Yours sincerely

Alison Standish
Small Business Training Co-ordinator

SkillShare
The Community & Youth Network
for Employment & Training

Member of the
National ITeC Network
Project of the
Westgate Community
Initiatives Group Inc.

Anh Vo

ROYAL CHILDREN'S HOSPITAL

Presented to _____ *Mr Anh Ngoc Vo* _____
in recognition of a significant contribution to the Good Friday Appeal for the Royal Children's Hospital

Appeal Director
Date *April 25, 1999*
Number *15*

Successfully Changing Lives by Building a Community

Quay West Precinct
5/71 Moreland Street, Footscray 3011 Phone (03) 9697 9563 Fax (03) 9689 0963

7th October 1996

Mr Anh Vo
4 Gibbs Street
MAIDSTONE VIC 3012

Dear Anh ,

Thank you for your offer of assistance on the final Sounding Board panel for the current NEIS program at Western Metropolitan Institute of TAFE (WMIT).

I enclose a brief profile of the applicants undertaking the course.

Also enclosed is a map and parking ticket which must be displayed on your dashboard.

I look forward to seeing you on Tuesday 15th October 1996 at

Yours sincerely

Beth Graham
NEIS Co-ordinator

143

Anh Vo

LIONS CLUB OF FOOTSCRAY
CHARTERED FEBRUARY 1963
DISTRICT 201 V 2 AUSTRALIA
6th CLUB IN AUSTRALIA

WE SERVE

Mr. George Eliades,
3 Charles Street.
Footscray. 3011.
Vic.

Secretary:

3rd. October, 1994.

Frank Hollingsworth,
P.O.Box 689.
Bacchus Marsh. 3340.
Vic.

TO WHOM IT MAY CONCERN

Dear Sir/Madam,

It affords me great pleasure to introduce Mr. Ahn Vo to you and
forward a reference as to his personal atributes.
Speaking as secretary and a fellow Lion, I have no doubts that
Ahn is a person of high principles and most dedicated in any
project undertaken by him for the benefit of Lionism and the
community in general.
Ahn is very industious in all his undertakings, whether it be in
business or in a private endeavour, completely trustworthy and
I have no hesitation, personally and on behalf of the Lions Club
of Footscray thoroughly endorsing Ahn to be accepted into any
enterprise he aspires to be involved in.

Yours sincerely,

Frank Hollingsworth.
Secretary.

PLEASE ADDRESS ALL CORRESPONDENCE TO THE SECRETARY

This book is my way of saying thank you and that I am deeply grateful for what this country has given me and that is why I am so passionate about making sure we keep our country of Australia safe and a beautiful place to live with no dishonestly or harmful ways, just love and peace for all.

www.ingramcontent.com/pod-product-compliance
Lightning Source LLC
Chambersburg PA
CBHW061327220326
41599CB00026B/5072